PSYCHOLOGY RESEARCH PROGRESS

GROUP THERAPY

THEORY, PRACTICES AND EFFECTIVENESS

Psychology Research Progress

Additional books in this series can be found on Nova's website under the Series tab.

Additional e-books in this series can be found on Nova's website under the e-book tab.

PSYCHOLOGY RESEARCH PROGRESS

GROUP THERAPY

THEORY, PRACTICES AND EFFECTIVENESS

HELLEN DERRICKSON
EDITOR

nova publishers
New York

Additional color graphics may be available in the e-book version of this book.

Library of Congress Cataloging-in-Publication Data

Group therapy : theory, practices and effectiveness / Editors: Hellen Derrickson.
pages cm. -- (Psychology research progress)
Includes index.
ISBN 978-1-63463-173-0 (hardcover)
1. Group psychotherapy. I. Derrickson, Hellen, editor.
RC488.G736 2014
616.89'152--dc23
2014037736

Published by Nova Science Publishers, Inc. † New York

Contents

PREFACE

As the power of talk therapy was beginning to be discovered, it became clear at about the same time that it was very difficult to provide individual therapy for many people at the same time. Such therapy was extremely time-consuming and costly of human energy. This book reviews group therapies, personal growth groups, and support groups. It discusses the theories, practices and effectiveness of group therapy.

Chapter 1 – Across societies and cultures, there exists a primary inborn healthy structure of the psyche, almost instinctual, that drives the unfolding process of individuals into healthy psychological functioning on four levels: needs, wants, rights, and decisions. In earlier stages of development, a child has some basic psychological needs that have to be met by his/her caregivers unconditionally, for his/her own (not their) sake and in an attitude-based not situation-based manner, such as the need to be loved, the need to be recognized, and the need to be accepted. These needs are bi-directional, i.e. the need to be loved is accompanied by the need to love. These needs are crucial to the healthy development of children and also influence adult behavior. It is postulated that a need that is not adequately met early in life, an expected deficiency in the corresponding healthy capacity might ensue in adulthood (Deficit model of psychopathology). Moreover, a need that was met during childhood usually continues into adulthood, but in a mild, adult, and appropriate form (Earley, 2002). At a later stage of development, not only the person knows what he or she is ought to do or should do, but also knows what he or she wants to do without having impeding fears or difficulties. The distinction between 'need' and 'want' is important here. A 'need' is an inborn natural drive common to all humans, that the author's can either 'want' or not. With further development, the person becomes consciously aware of basic psychological rights to have own basic psychological needs satisfied, such as the right to feel worthy, to make mistakes, or to be happy, and having the willingness to get these rights. The next level is decisions, when now the person is fully aware of his freedom to choose, to decide and to act in the direction of his basic psychological needs. He or she also has the ability to take responsibility for his choices, decisions and actions.

Chapter 2 – As the power of talk therapies were beginning to be discovered, it became clear at about the same time that it was very difficult to provide individual therapy for many people. Such therapy was extremely time-consuming and costly of human energy. This chapter will review the group therapies, personal growth groups, and support groups.

Chapter 3 – The author's qualitative study explores the dynamics, phenomena, and processes occurring in 12 older people's closed groups, which were arranged as a psychosocial group intervention for older adults suffering from loneliness. The groups were formed to alleviate loneliness. The authors aimed to reduce the heterogeneity of participants during recruitment. Individuals with significant dementia, mobility disability, or sensory deficits were therefore excluded. The group programs were arranged according to participant interests so as to ensure that individuals with similar interests would be grouped together (art, exercise). All groups included 7–8 participants (N=93; females n=68, mean age 80) and they met once a week on 12 occasions (6 hours/day) during three months. All groups had two professional group facilitators.

The authors used three different types of data and grounded theory to explore the occurring group processes: 1) facilitators' detailed descriptions from each group meeting (ca. 300 pages); 2) researchers' observations and field notes of group visits (two/each group); 3) participants' feedback of the groups.

Each group went through a common path from one stage to another: from initial chaos to an effectively working and self-directed group. The entire life course was experienced by 11/12 groups, although differences were observed in development speed. Other special characteristics were detected in the lonely older people's groups. Some are features typical of all older people's groups (diseases, heterogenic functional status), and some are probably typical for only these types of loneliness groups (difficulties in adhering to their group, reluctance to discuss feelings of loneliness), art groups (courage to try new things with peer support, avoiding conversations about diseases), exercise groups (eroticism, competition between group members), and some phenomena might be specific for several group types (flirting, a common secret between group members, a common enemy increasing group cohesion). Participants had some common group roles in these groups (e.g. leader, critic, silent, dominant, team spirit creator, disabled).

Group dynamics and group roles in older people's groups resemble those known from adult groups. However, some features are different and could be taken into account when planning and gathering therapeutic groups for older people.

Chapter 4 – *Background:* Rehabilitation in musculoskeletal disorders through group treatment is commonly cited in literature, especially so in the last ten years, despite the fact that the contents and the characteristics of these programs are poorly documented.

The aims of this chapter are: 1) to perform a narrative review on the cognitive behavioral approach and on group treatments for chronic low back pain (LBP), 2) to propose a "multimodal group program" model and to explain its application in different chronic spinal dysfunctions and diseases (disc degeneration, arthritis, spinal stenosis, anatomical and clinical instability), and 3) to show an example of this type of group treatment.

Methods: A narrative review of literature was performed on the basis of current evidence. The "multimodal group program" proposal was based on recent knowledge about the mechanical, neurophysiological and behavioral components of chronic spinal pain.

Finally, methods for the practical example were the following:

Sample: six subjects with chronic LBP (lasting at least three months)

Treatment: 10 weekly one-hour sessions

Outcome measures: Numerical Rating Scale (NRS), Oswestry Disability Index – Italian Version (ODI –I), Roland & Morris Disability Questionnaire (RMDQ), Tampa Scale for Kinesiophobia (TSK), and Short-Form Health Survey Questionnaire (SF-36)

Timing: outcome measures were administered at baseline and at the end of the ten sessions.

Discussion: The group treatment the authors proposed is defined as "multimodal" because during each meeting, a physical therapist incorporates some specific exercises with information and practical training on correct postures and movements. Moreover, explanation about the mechanisms for onset and persistence of pain and about the different strategies to manage it (through exercise, relaxation and active coping strategies) is a fundamental part of the program.

This group treatment includes different physical therapy strategies (joint mobilization, muscle strengthening, coordination and balance exercises, stretching, and so on) and a psychological approach, to modify beliefs and behaviors and to reduce the need for individual treatment.

Chapter 5 – In this chapter, the author overviewed the application of collaborative LEGO® block creation and examined its psychological effects. First, previous studies concerned with collaborative LEGO® block creation were reviewed.

Secondly the effect of the creation, especially in social skills and trust, was examined. Third, the effect of the collaborative creation, in the sense of being accepted by others, was also examined. These results indicate that collaborative work facilitates social skills and the division of roles, positively affecting the sense of acceptance, and presenting a new possibility for the application of block creation in the field of group therapy. Finally, the authors introduced the practices of collaborative LEGO® block creation based on these studies. This group work is also effective for children with developmental disorders, such as autism, and groups requiring cross-cultural communication.

Chapter 6 – This study involved the use of a short session of Emotional Freedom Techniques (EFT) with two English ladies soccer teams.

It is a randomised controlled trial with a supporting uncontrolled trial.

It was designed to verify the results of an earlier similar American trial involving basketball players.

The results show a significant improvement in goal scoring ability from a dead ball situation following a short EFT session. These results support those of the earlier trial.

In: Group Therapy
Editor: Hellen Derrickson

ISBN: 978-1-63463-173-0

Chapter 1

The Four-Step Integrative Model for Group Psychotherapy: Description, Development and Application in Egyptian Culture

Refaat Mahfouz, M.D., Mohamed Taha, M.D., and Waguih William IsHak, M.D.
FAPA, Washington, D.C., US

"Behind every overt psychological symptom or difficulty, there is a covert un-met psychological need."

Introduction

Across societies and cultures, there exists a primary inborn healthy structure of the psyche, almost instinctual, that drives the unfolding process of individuals into healthy psychological functioning on four levels: needs, wants, rights, and decisions. In earlier stages of development, a child has some basic psychological needs that have to be met by his/her caregivers unconditionally, for his/her own (not their) sake and in an attitude-based not situation-based manner, such as the need to be loved, the need to be recognized, and the need to be accepted. These needs are bi-directional, i.e. the need to be loved is accompanied by the need to love. These needs are crucial to the healthy development of children and also influence adult behavior. It is postulated that a need that is not adequately met early in life, an expected deficiency in the corresponding healthy capacity might ensue in adulthood (Deficit model of psychopathology). Moreover, a need that was met during childhood usually continues into adulthood, but in a mild, adult, and appropriate form (Earley, 2002). At a later stage of development, not only the person knows what he or she is ought to do or should do, but also knows what he or she wants to do without having impeding fears or difficulties. The distinction between 'need' and 'want' is important here. A 'need' is an inborn natural drive common to all humans, that we can either 'want' or not. With further development, the person becomes consciously aware of basic psychological rights to have own basic psychological needs satisfied, such as the right to feel worthy, to make mistakes, or to be happy, and having the willingness to get these rights. The next level is decisions, when now the person is fully aware of his freedom to choose, to decide and to act in the direction of his basic psychological needs. He or she also has the ability to take responsibility for his choices, decisions and actions.

The Four-Step Integrative Model Theoretical Background

We are all born with some basic psychological needs. In order to have one's own psychological needs met, a child might have to accept what his parents say and do to him, even by accepting the parents blockade of own actions for fear of abandonment and withdrawal of love (Becker, 1993). The child's needs are confronted with the parents' wants, therefore, a real conflict emerges. This conflict is then internalized, so when the child wants to get his or her own need met, he or she fears that one's own want (will/action to have the need met) would irritate his parents and cause them to punish or withdraw their love. Subsequently, wants become accompanied by inner fears leading to discomfort and distress (Conflict model of psychopathology). After many unsuccessful trials to express or enact 'wants' to have the psychological need met, the child now gives up the right to fulfill that need, in order not to get in trouble and just live in peace. Finally, the child decides to be compliant and adaptive to the overwhelming parental demands and develops a pattern corresponding to the parents' expectations, i.e., giving up one's own needs and conforming to others' own wants. In Winnicott's (1965) terminology, the child buries his or her *true self* and develops a *false self* in order to adapt to the parental and environmental pressures. In Eric Bern's transactional analysis understanding, the child turns his or her *Free* Child Ego State into an *Adapted* Child Ego State by taking some early decisions in response to the parents' injunctions and counter-injunctions, in order to survive physically and psychologically (Goulding and Goulding, 1978 and 1979).

A child with an invalidated need to be recognized might decide to lead the life of a schizoid, avoidant or dependent person. Or, on the contrary, one may decide to do everything to be seen and recognized and turns to be a histrionic. Moreover, one may decide not to believe anyone who recognizes him or her based on being drawn to think that one is not worth recognition. These *early decisions* may have been appropriate in certain situations in childhood, but are inappropriate in adulthood. So, in due course, this person might be seeking psychiatric help. Of course things are not that simple and direct. Many psychological, genetic, situational, socio-cultural and environmental factors interplay to favor one decision or the other. We can comprehend a number of psychiatric disorders in the light of this understanding, which relates every overt psychological symptom or difficulty to a covert un-met psychological need.

It always starts with a basic psychological need, the wanting of which gets accompanied by many fears, leading to giving up the right to have the need met, ending by an inevitable maladaptive decision. Clinically, we can see patients at different levels of unhealthy psychological functioning in correspondence to the described assumptions:

- On the level of needs: Patients either deny or intensify their basic psychological needs, because these needs have been actually denied or not met by their parents or caregivers.
- On the level of wants: Patients know what they ought to do but do not know or afraid to know what they want to do, as their parenting style was full of 'oughts, 'musts' and 'shoulds', such as "you must succeed", "you ought to be polite", or "you should be strong", without explicit inclusion of children's own wants. If they permit themselves to want, many fears and doubts are expected to evolve.
- On the level of rights: Patients are not aware of their psychological rights, simply because they have not been granted those rights or have not given the chance to get them.

- On the level of decisions: Patients who have taken maladaptive decisions and have chosen to live maladaptive life scripts.

THE FOUR-STEP INTEGRATIVE MODEL PSYCHOTHERAPEUTIC TECHNIQUE

The Four Steps

Just like the described psychopathological process, the psychotherapeutic process runs along four hierarchical steps. The first step is to encourage the client to identify the basic psychological *need* behind his behavior or symptom and to find a healthy rationale(s) for fullfilling that need. Earley (2002) suggests that in psychotherapy it is helpful to identify basic interpersonal needs that are central to human motivation.

The second step in the described model is to help the person express the *want*/will for having his psychological need met, and explore the inner fears that block him from doing so (the fears that he or she has acquired during childhood, i.e., becoming consciously aware of inner conflicts. In line with this, Yalom (1980) wonders how often therapists work with patients who decide that it is better not to want. For them, wanting makes one vulnerable or leaves one exposed.

The third step is to help the patient become consciously aware of the *right* to have own needs met and explore the real or imagined obstacles expected to be overcome in the way.

This step can correlate to Yalom's (1980) notice that many people do not permit themselves many rights (e.g. the right to wish), as though their wishing would irritate, threaten, or drive away others.

The fourth step is to help the person *decide* to develop a new (healthy) pattern of behavior that corresponds to one's true self rather than the false self, undoing the maladaptive decisions picked up during childhood. Decision is the bridge between wishing and acting. To decide means to commit oneself to a course of action. No change is possible without effort, and decision is the trigger of effort (Yalom, 1980).

Therapeutic work on each step can last for several sessions until the therapist and the patient determine together that it is time to move to the next step.

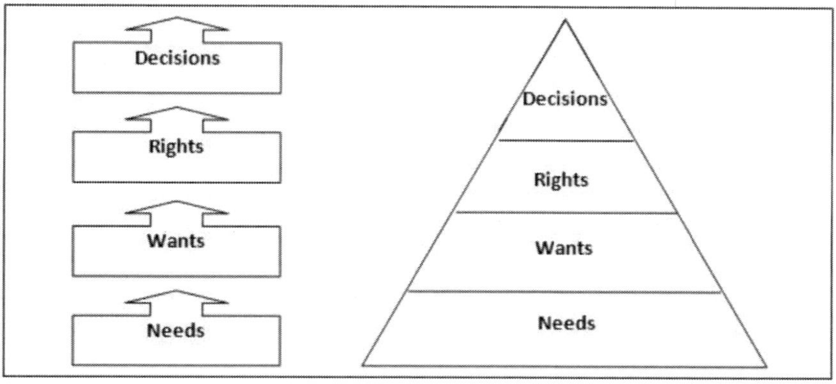

The Four-step Integrative Model for Group Psychotherapy works hierarchically on levels of patients' needs, wants, rights and decisions.

Technique Application and Examples

Clinically, the four-step integrative model for group psychotherapy hierarchically targets the mentioned four levels of psychological functioning (needs, wants, rights and decisions) via what is called “the four-step therapeutic game” (Mahfouz and Taha, 2011). This is a simple technique derived from an integrative combination of several gestalt games (well known group psychotherapy techniques devised to foster immediacy of awareness) (Bateman et al., 2000). This technique is designed to run in four steps, each step corresponds to one level of psychological functioning. In practicing this therapeutic technique/game in the here and now, a patient is asked to complete the missing part of a sentence -suggested by the therapist- with several different responses. The patient is advised to direct his speech to a different group member each and every time he speaks. The given examples are intentionally simplified to clarify the basic practice of the model. However, the original excerpts have more details such as group members’ difficulties initiating the therapeutic work, feedback by other group members, and suggestions/modifications of technique practice.

The four steps of the technique/game as applied in clinical practice are formulated as follows:

1. I need...Because/in order to... (Completed by group member)

2. I want...But I am afraid that... (Completed by group member).
3. It is my right to..Even if/in spite of... (Completed by group member).
4. I decide...and I take responsibility for it.

Examples

1. I need to accept myself as a whole, in order to stop blaming myself.
   OR
2. I need to accept myself as a whole, because I have never been accepted as a whole.
3. I want to accept myself as a whole, but I am afraid that other people don't accept me.
4. It is my right to accept myself as a whole, even if many people don't accept me.
   OR
5. It is my right to accept myself as a whole, in spite of my current failures.
6. I decide to accept myself as a whole, and I take responsibility for it.

The following are detailed examples from real group therapy sessions, held in Minia University Hospital, Egypt for adult female patients (Upper Egyptian subculture imposes separation of men and women in variable social situations, however, male trainees and co-therapists can attend). This is an open continuous outpatient large group. Patients can participate in this group provided that they are adult females, under regular follow up by staff of Minia University psychiatry department. Patients carry heterogeneous diagnoses, excluding those in active psychotic or manic episodes. Sessions are held once weekly for 90 minutes.

Example 1

Patient: Dr. Refaat (the therapist), I don't feel that I am loved by any one!

Therapist: … Do you believe that you deserve to be loved?

Patient: No.

………………………………………………………………………………

Therapist: I suggest you try working on: "I need to believe that I deserve to be loved, in order to…"

Patient (Directing her words to group members):

- (Trainee 1), I need to believe that I deserve to be loved, in order to…mm... *stop mutilating myself.*
- (Patient 2), I need to believe that I deserve to be loved, in order to *stop leading men on.*
- (Trainee 3), I need to believe that I deserve to be loved, in order to *feel my true inner power.*

Example 2

Patient: I am a bad person! I have many failures.

Therapist: We all have failures! I have many failures too. Without failures we never learn.

Patient: I need to *challenge* myself and *fight* my failures. Would you help me, please?

Therapist: You don't have to challenge yourself, and you are not supposed to fight a part of yourself. Failure is a part of every human's nature.

Patient: Then what?

………………………………………………………………………………………

Therapist: I suggest you try playing "I need to accept my failures, because…"

Patient: But I don't want to accept my failures, I will not play this game!

Therapist: You don't *wan*t to, but you may *need* to. Let's try; it is just a game...

Patient: Ok. I need to accept my failures, because…I don't find words, help me…

Therapist: Because I am a human being.

Patient: Yes, I need to accept my failures because I am a human being.

………………………………………………………………………………………

- (Patient 2), I need to accept my failures because...mm…because I don't like to be that sad forever.
- (Trainee 3), I need to accept my failures, because every person may have failures.

Therapist: Well done, thank you. Anybody else would like to try this game?

Example 3

Therapist (to patient in example 2): Few weeks ago you worked on "I *need* to accept my failures because…" Now I am suggesting you try working on "I *want* to accept my failures, but I am afraid that…" What do you think?

Patient: Yes... I really need to accept my failures and to accept myself as a whole, but I don't know why I can't do that, I am stuck.

Therapist: In therapy, "*I can't*" means "*I don't want*". And "*I don't want*" means "*I want but I am afraid that…*" you may give it a try...

Patient: Ok.

- (Trainee 1), I want to accept my failures, but I am afraid that they are too many.
- (Patient 2), I want to accept my failures, but I am afraid that I will have to accept myself.
- (Patient 2): I think it's time to accept yourself.

Trainee: Yes.

- (Patient 3), I want to accept my failures, but I am afraid that you don't accept them.
- (Patient 3): But I accept you as a whole, including your failures.

Example 4

Therapist (to patient of example 2): Do you feel that you have the right to accept your failures?

Patient: Nobody has given me this right before! Is it my right to do so?

Therapist: Of course it is. You have been given this right by Allah (God). Your parents might have taken it from you. Now it is time for you to re-own it and let nobody take it from you again.

Patient: I am not sure of that.

Therapist: After the work you have done in the past few months, you are aware that you need to accept your failures, and you are also aware of the fears that block you from wanting so. Do you think it is time to work on your right to accept your failures?

Patient: I think I am ready.

Therapist: OK, let's try: "It is my right to accept my failures, even if/in spite of …"

Patient: It is my right to accept my failures, even if nobody accepted them.

- (Patient 5): It is my right to accept my failures, even if they are too many.
- (Co-therapist): It is my right to accept my failures, in spite of all my fears.
- (Co-therapist): It is my right to accept my failures too.

Example 5

Therapist (to patient of example 2): Would you like to take a step forwards?

Patient: Yes, please!

Therapist: Let's decide it, decide to accept your failures, and be responsible for your decision.

....

Patient: Well, I decide to accept my failures, and I take responsibility for this decision in front of myself, in front of you and in front of Allah.

Therapist: It is your right to decide this.

Patient: Yes.

- (Trainee 2), I decide to accept my failures, and I take responsibility for this decision in front of myself, in front of you and in front of Allah.
- (Trainee 2): I share you in your decision for myself.
- Patient: Good for you doctor… (All laugh).
- (Patient 3), I decide to accept my failures, and I take responsibility for this decision in front of myself, in front of you and in front of Allah.
- (Patient 3): I am happy for you!
- Patient: I am happy too.
- (Trainee 3), I decide to accept my failures, and I take responsibility for this decision in front of myself, in front of you and in front of Allah.
- (Trainee 3): Remember that you are responsible for your decision forever.

DEVELOPMENT AND VALIDATION OF THE FOUR-STEP INTEGRATIVE MODEL

In the mid seventies of the last century in Egypt, group therapy was developed by Yehia Rakhawy who is considered with Mohamed Shaalan as the chief founders of group therapy in Egypt. This model was developed in the context of the Arabic language, the Islamic tradition, Egyptian folk traditions, and the importance of harmonizing with one's 'biorhythmic natural surroundings' (Rakhawy, 1978 and 1994). Rakhawy's model for conducting group therapy would best be described as a synthesis between Existential philosophy orientation, Object relations theory, Gestalt techniques and Transactional Analysis, with the finger prints of its originator and conductor remarkably all through (Ghoz, 1977).

About three decades later, Refaat Mahfouz extended Rakhawy's model to Upper Egypt by integrating more theoretical and clinical elements, and developed what is now known as "The Four-step Integrative Model for Group Psychotherapy". Mahfouz, who was trained in Dar El-Mokattam Mental Health Hospital in Cairo by Yehia Rakhawy, implemented most of the theoretical and clinical constituents of Rakhawy's model, but later incorporated more theoretical components, practical techniques and socio-cultural orientations into the model. His original intention was not only to conduct a therapy group in Upper Egypt, but also to integrate this relatively new approach into a larger training and research scheme. As shown in research studies, this model, like its precursor, draws its basic constructs from many schools of psychological thought: psychoanalysis (Mohamed, 2008), object relations theory (Kamal, 2002 and 2007 and Abd El-Na'em, 2013), self psychology (Saleh, 2001), transactional analysis (Ebrahim, 2006), Gestalt therapy (Taha, 2003), re-decision therapy (Aly, 2004), cognitive behavioral therapy (ElSerogy, 2006) and existential psychotherapy (Yousof, 2008) in a creative integrative manner that is deeply influenced by the local cultural and social norms and expectations (Taha and Mahfouz, 2008). The model defines some therapeutic *values* (that are universal to any group therapy approach in any culture; e.g. confidentiality and non-judgmental attitude, some therapeutic *norms* (that are culture-specific; e.g. time flexibility, religious restraints and common social traditions) and some therapeutic *rules* (that are model-specific; e.g. here and now, I-thou, no gossiping, and no shoulds). The model provides an example of how group psychotherapy can be tailored to a certain society/culture.

The first structured therapy group in Upper Egypt was held in Minia University hospital, July 2000 and only included adult males with different diagnostic categories except for patients with active psychotic or manic episodes. The inner active group circle included 15 members: 10 patients, 4 trainees, and the group leader. The rest of the trainees were included in an outer circle as actively observing participants. One year later, a group for adult female patients was formed and its first session included 14 female patients having the same previously mentioned inclusion criteria. Simultaneously, another group for adolescent patients was also formed and had its first session with 5 patients. On May 2002, the first diagnosis-specific therapy group was established, and its first session included 6 borderline female patients and 5 trainees.

Many research studies were conducted to study various clinical and theoretical aspects of this group therapy training program. An earlier one (Taha, 2003) was designed to study the structure, functions and classification of "Gestalt Games", which was the mainly used therapeutic technique in the program. This study defined four hierarchical levels of working through clients' psychological difficulties: needs, wants, rights and decisions, and investigated the use of a four-step therapeutic technique. Further academic and clinical development performed by Minia team of group therapists laid the basis for the theoretical framework based on the ongoing clinical experience, culminating into the approach now known as "The Four-step Integrative Model for Group Psychotherapy". This model is becoming more and more known, practiced and trained upon in various scientific circles and encounters, including American Group Psychotherapy Association (AGPA)'s annual meeting for the last 3 years.

THE APPLICATION OF THE FOUR-STEP INTEGRATIVE MODEL TO EGYPTIAN CULTURE

Different cultures don't only have different views about what a person is, but also different views about what the project of psychotherapy is. Maybe there would be agreement that what a human being is, depends on the culture she/he grows up in and in which she/he lives (Hinshelwood, 2010). Cultures affect the way persons lead lives, and therefore they also affect the nature of psychotherapy itself, which aims to facilitate new strategies for patients and clients. Moreover, Different cultures inevitably define a different role for the therapist and group leader (Hinshelwood, 2008).

For millennia, Egypt maintained a strikingly complex and stable culture that influenced later cultures of Europe, the Middle East and Africa. After the Pharaonic era, Egypt came under the influence of Hellenism, for a time, Christianity and later, Arab and Islamic culture. The Egyptian culture is mainly derived from the interplay of three key factors: family, language, and religion (Badalto, 1984). The four-step integrative model for group psychotherapy is a natural product of such interplay. As described and exemplified above, the four-step model is directive, quite prescriptive and seems to operate at level of conscious awareness and conscious will more than unconscious group process and group dynamics. It doesn't use "interpretation", but rather "actualization of interpretation" through living a new here and now experience of bringing into conscious awareness what is unconscious (Rakhawy, personal communication, May 1st, 1975). The model is characterized by a directive leadership style, an active group psychotherapeutic technique, a psycho-educational trend and an integration of the spiritual/religious dimension into the therapeutic work as detailed below.

Directive Leadership Style

On the continuum of active/directive/prescriptive versus passive/non-directive/descriptive leadership, Taha et al. (2008 and 2010) concluded that the style of leading most therapy groups in Egypt is more towards the active/directive/prescriptive pole. The leader in the four-step model is interested not only in behavior and its unconscious meaning, but also the quality of presence and contact as each group member explores his or her own self and interact with each other. The leader may ask questions to elicit patients' awareness of their experience in the moment and the deeper issues that underlie their reactions. The group leader sometimes makes suggestions about new behavior or attitudes that patients can try experimentally. When necessary, the leader actively intervenes to make sure that the group is safe enough for members and is moving in a therapeutic direction. Sometimes, the leader doesn't wait for the group work to emerge gradually but actively encourages it. Other times, the leader makes an internal shift in attitude moving from a leader-centered to a group-centered mode (Earley's, 2002). Such leadership style is attributed to socio-cultural factors of Egyptian culture

(Taha et al., 2008), such as the Role of the Parent, the Unconscious Image of the Leader, and the Aim of Psychotherapy.

One of the major socio-cultural differences between Western and Egyptian (Arabic-Islamic) cultures is that Western cultures emphasizes self-sufficiency, independence from family and self-growth while Egyptian people value interdependence more than independence, social consciousness more than individual freedom, and the welfare of the group more than their own. In Egypt, family roles tend to be highly structured and obligations to parents are highly respected throughout one's life. The family structure is traditionally patriarchal in that communication and authority flow vertically from top to bottom. Parents are afforded a great deal of esteem that might reach some grade of holiness, and this respect governs interpersonal interactions. Hence, certain characters of the traditional Egyptian father figure are expected to be displayed by the group leader/father in a therapeutic setting when the group is led by male leader. Among those characteristics, being present, interactive, directive, intellectually and emotionally involved, interested in group members' everyday life details, and protective. With regards to the Egyptian social unconscious image of a leader, a psychotherapy group leader in the Egyptian community is drawn to play the role of a prophet or a religious teacher, who teaches, instructs, directs and prescribes besides providing care, acceptance, understanding and unconditional love to his followers. The role of history and religion is obvious here (Taha, 2014). On one hand, fathers and ancestors were held high above questioning and criticism since the times of the Pharaohs. On the other hand, religion in the Egyptian society is often a pervasive force governing behavior. Egyptians typically place a high value on spiritual matters and religion. Most therapy groups in Egypt call for the inclusion of moral discourse in the aim and practice of psychotherapy and the cultivation in therapists of the virtues and skills needed to be moral consultants to their clients. This has drawn most Egyptian group leaders to play a particular directive, guiding and prescriptive role. The issues of moral responsibility and community well-being are always present in the four-step model, and a carefully balanced attention to these issues is believed to have the ability to greatly expand the contribution of psychotherapy to the alleviation of the Egyptian community problems.

Active Group Psychotherapeutic Technique

Some psychotherapy techniques might work better in specific cultures or communities than others. Social and cultural norms clearly affect how individuals experience their emotions. Egyptian people (as part of the Middle Eastern culture) tend to experience and express emotions passionately. They are deeply affected with and stirred by emotions. They intensively express their feelings such as anger, love, grief, jealousy, openly and without social restraints. Accordingly, the psyche of people in cultures that is accepting more emotionality might be better accessed by techniques that involve emotional ventilation and stirring up (e.g. psychodrama and Gestalt games) to be more in touch with oneself and others, while the psyche of people in cultures that emphasize intellectuality might be better accessed by techniques that involve intellectual mental work, for better understanding of self and others (e.g. interpretation).

Another factor that favors using active group techniques is that most therapy groups in Egypt are large in size due to the high population density in relation to introduced psychotherapeutic service. Working in large groups need some balance between increasing awareness and introspection while structuring the group through a natural positive leader (De Maré, 1975, cited in Weinberg, 2006).

Psycho-Educational Role of the Four-Step Model in Egyptian Culture

Only 72 percent of the total Egyptian population can read and write. Currently, many governmental and non-governmental organizations invest in efforts to increase knowledge and awareness among the Egyptian general public.

Psychological language and terminology is not as common and familiar in the Egyptian culture as in the case with Western societies. The four-step model plays an influential role in helping patients develop not their own psychological knowledge and awareness, but more importantly recognize and be consciously aware of their needs, wants and rights. It also helps people take responsibility for their choices, decisions and actions.

Integration of the Spiritual/Religious Dimension in Four-Step Model in Egypt

At least three of the world's major religions – Judaism, Christianity, and Islam – can trace their roots and/or early dissemination to the land of the Nile. Most of the known prophets have spent some parts of their life journeys in Egypt, or at least left their footprints beneath its land. The role of religion in the Egyptian society is often a pervasive force governing behavior. Egyptians typically place a high value on spiritual matters and religion.

Egyptian culture supplants religion as the accepted guide and reference for human conduct. In this context, it is acceptable and sometimes desirable to integrate the spiritual/religious dimension in Egyptian therapy group work, where the group leader becomes the *de facto* moral and religious teacher (Taha et al., 2008).

THE FOUR-STEP MODEL AND OTHER CULTURES

The Four-Step Integrative Model for Group Psychotherapy is a good example of how group psychotherapy can be adjusted to a collectivist culture. The model fits the Egyptian culture well through a structured group, with an emphasis on direct and active interventions of the group leader which suits the hierarchical structure of Egyptian society and the need for an active leadership, all with a psycho-educational component that teaches the members about their needs, rights and responsibilities (Weinberg, personal communication, September 3rd, 2013). Although the Four-Step Integrative Model has been presented as a half-day workshop and was very well received in the AGPA's annual meetings of 2012, 2013 and 2014, there are no studies that investigate its use in other cultures yet. However, it seems that the hierarchy of needs, wants, rights and decisions is a universal one that can be worked through in different cultures by different therapeutic approaches; the four-step model is one of them. We look forward to conduct research on the use of the four-step model in cultures other than the Egyptian one.

REFERENCES

Abd El-Na'em, M. M. (2013). [Object relations in dynamic interactive group psychotherapy: Principles and practice]. Unpublished raw data.

Ahlin, G. (2010). Activity versus passivity in conductor styles: Further reflections about Egyptian and Group-Analytic conductor styles in group psychotherapy. *Group Analysis*, 43(2), 185–189.

Aly, M. K. (2004). Redecision in group treatment as applied in dynamic interactive therapy groups. Unpublished master's thesis, faculty of medicine, Mina University, Minia, Egypt.

Badalto, E. (1984). Learning to think like an Arab Muslim: A short guide to understanding the Arab mentality'. Retrieved from http:// www.blackwaterusa.com/btw2004/articles/0503arabs.html

Bateman, A., Brown, D. and Pedder, J. (2000). Introduction to psychotherapy. An outline of psychodynamic principles and practice. London: Routledge.

Becker, E. (1993). Growing up rugged: Fritz Perls and gestalt therapy. Gestalt Journal, 16(2), 123-134.

Earley, J. (2002). Interactive group therapy: Integrating interpersonal, action-oriented, and psychodynamic approaches. Philadelphia: Brunner/Mazel.

Ebrahim, A. Z. (2006). Ego states theory : implications in psychotherapy. Unpublished master's thesis, faculty of medicine, Mina University, Minia, Egypt.

ElSerogy, Y. (2006). Principles of cognitive behavioral therapy in dynamic interactive therapy groups. Unpublished doctoral thesis, faculty of medicine, Assiut University, Assiut, Egypt.

Ghoz, E. H. (1977). Group Psychotherapy: A dynamic study of an Egyptian Approach. Unpublished master's thesis, faculty of medicine, Cairo University, Cairo, Egypt.

Goulding, R. and Goulding, M. (1978). The power is in the patient: A TA/Gestalt approach to psychotherapy. San Francisco: TA Press.

Goulding, R. and Goulding, M. (1979). Changing lives through redecision therapy. New York: Brunner/Mazel.

Hinshelwood, R. D. (2008). Forwards. In M. Taha and R. Mahfouz (Eds.), Psychotherapy as a creative process: theoretical and clinical perspectives (first edition, pp 9-14). Saarbrücken, Germany: VDM Verlag.

Hinshelwood, R. D. (2010). Comment on "Power of love and love of power in group psychotherapy" by Mohammed Taha et al. *Group Analysis*, 43(2), 181-184.

Kamal, A. M. (2002). Psychotherapy alliance in a therapy group. Unpublished master's thesis, faculty of medicine, Minia University, Minia, Egypt.

Kamal, A. M. (2007). The concept of bisexuality according to object-relations theory: Therapeutic approach in dynamic interactive group treatment. Unpublished doctoral thesis, faculty of medicine, Mina University, Minia, Egypt.

Mahfouz, R., and Taha, M. (2011). The four levels therapeutic game: A new approach for facilitating therapeutic change. In D. Bloom and P. Brownell (Eds.), Continuity and change: Gestalt therapy now (first edition, pp 203-220). Newcastle, England: Cambridge scholars publishing.

Mittscherlich, A. (1963). Society without the father: A contribution to social psychology. New York: Harcourt Brace and World.

Mohamed, T. A. (2008). Transference phenomena in group psychotherapy: An analytic study in a dynamic interactive therapy group. Unpublished doctoral thesis, faculty of medicine, Minia University, Minia, Egypt.

Pines, M. (2010). Comment on Taha et al.'s 'Power of Love and Love of Power'. *Group Analysis*, 43(2): 190–191.

Punter, J. (2009). Not Group Analysis as we know it: Response to Mohamed Taha,. Refaat Mahfouz and Magdy Arafa's `Socio-Cultural Influences on Group Therapy Leadership Style. *Group Analysis*, 42(1):80–87.

Punter, J. (2010). Group Analysis as I do It: How I work with the social unconscious. *Group Analysis*, 43(2), 170–180.

Rakhawy, Y. T. (1978). Introduction in group psychotherapy. Cairo, Egypt: Dar Al Ghad.

Rakhawy, Y. T. (1994). Madness, creativity and society. *Journal of Comparative Poetics,* 14, 206–27.

Saleh. R. S. (2001). Principles of self psychology as applied in an integrative dynamic therapy group. Unpublished master's thesis, faculty of medicine, Minia University, Minia.

Taha, M. (2003). Gestalt games in group psychotherapy: Analysis of structure and functions. Unpublished master's thesis, faculty of medicine, Minia University, Minia, Egypt.

Taha, M., Abd-El-Hameed, M. A., Kamal, A., Hasan, M. A., and Mahfouz, R. (2010). Power of love and love of power in group psychotherapy. *Group Analysis,* 43(2), 155-169.

Taha, M., and Mahfouz, R. (2008). Psychotherapy as a creative process: theoretical and clinical perspectives. Saarbrücken, Germany: VDM Verlag.

Taha, M., Mahfouz, R., and Arafa, M. (2008). Socio-cultural influence on group therapy leadership style. *Group Analysis*, 41(4), 391–406.

Taha, M. (2014). Social positions, scripts and functioning dynamics: Phenomenology of the Egyptian social unconscious. *International Journal of Group Psychotherapy,* 64(3),323-343.

Weinberg, H. (2006). Group Analysis, Large Groups, and the Internet Unconscious. Unpublished PhD thesis, Manchester Metropolitan University, Manchester, United Kingdom.

Winnicott, D. W. (1965). The maturational process and the facilitating environment: Studies in the theory of emotional development. New York: International UP Inc.

Yalom, I. D. (1980). Existential psychotherapy. NY: Basic Books.

Yousef, M. (2008). [Principles of existential psychotherapy in dynamic interactive therapy groups]. Unpublished raw data.

In: Group Therapy
Editor: Hellen Derrickson
ISBN: 978-1-63463-173-0

Chapter 2

Overview of Group Therapies, Personal Growth Groups and Support Groups: Theories and Research Support

Rebecca Coleman Curtis[1] and Afshan Ladha[1,2]
[1]Adelphi University and Faculty,
[2]WA White Institute, US

Abstract

As the power of talk therapies were beginning to be discovered, it became clear at about the same time that it was very difficult to provide individual therapy for many people. Such therapy was extremely time-consuming and costly of human energy. This chapter will review the group therapies, personal growth groups, and support groups.

History

In 1905 J. H. Pratt in Boston began to incorporate home visits, diaries and a weekly call of 25 patients into his treatment of tuberculosis. This treatment appeared to be quite useful in combatting the depression accompanying the illness. When Freud visited the US in 1909 he visited James Jackson Putnam at Putnam Camp (Prochnik, 2006) and must have learned of Putnam's views of the use of a benevolent community in psychiatric hospitals in improving mental disorders. Putnam was a founder of the American Psychoanalytic Association in 1911 and its first President. His use of groups was similar in some respects, to that of the Therapeutic Milieu or Therapeutic Community in psychiatric hospitals today. Alder, convinced of the necessity of people with problems in living focusing on the general social interest and helping others, began to use group counseling in his child guidance centers by the second decade of the twentieth century.

Moreno, in Vienna, had written of the importance of the idea of people meeting eye to eye and face to face. He published the *Invitation to Encounter* (1914-15), a precursor to the later movement of encounter groups for people without psychiatric problems. He was also responsible for development of the method of psychodrama, a procedure in which various individuals act out the parts of problematic people in the volunteer's life. In the United States, Trigant Burrow, who had heard the lectures of Freud and went for a one-year analysis with Jung, advocated the use of groups, but was expelled as a member of the American Psychoanalytic Association in 1932, of which he had been President in 1924-25 (Pertegato and Pertegato, 2013). This error was later corrected, however, when he was given the A. A. Brill Award. Burrow coined the term "group psychotherapy" (Scheidlinger, 1992) and was using groups by 1925. He also used the term "group analysis" (Pertegato and Pertegato, 2013), but due to his omission from the literature, was not often credited with this innovation until recently. Although Freud was initially appreciative of Burrow, Scheidlinger attributes Freud's own abandoning of his interest in groups to his dislike of Burrow's experiments with them. In the 1930's Paul Shilder applied group therapy to prison inmates and discharged patients from psychiatric hospitals and is credited with the development of the concept of the Therapeutic Community, although this concept appears to have evolved earlier.

World War II exacerbated the need for therapy for returning soldiers and the use of group therapy expanded. Wilfred Bion and S. H. Foulkes had developed in the UK at Northfield Hospital a treatment for those soldiers suffering from PTSD. Each later, at the Tavistock Institute in London,, developed their own particular style of group experience, with Foulkes establishing the Group Analytic Society in 1952 and as a Learned Society in 1956 (Brown, 1983). Bion eventually published his influential *Experiences in Groups* (1961). Meanwhile, in 1947, Kurt Lewin, a protégé of Moreno, by then at MIT, was asked by the state of Connecticut, after the passage of the Fair Employment Practice Act, along with the Office of Naval Research and the National Educational Association, to train leaders to help deal with tensions among ethnic groups. He began the National Training Laboratories and began what is known as the Training or T-Group. These groups were to train leaders and also to engage in sensitivity training. Hence, many social psychologists, and others, not trained as therapists, began to be involved in the group movement. Various groups, usually called Encounter Groups, began to spring up in many places in the United States in the 1960's, and traditional mental health practitioners, alarmed at the spread of untrained mental professionals leading such groups, had legislation passed to keep such groups out of schools and to hold leaders legally responsible for negative effects (Yalom and Leszcz, 2005).

Although many therapists initially thought of group treatment as a substitute for the more costly individual therapy, there were others who considered it superior for participants from its inception (Dies, 2003) and others who found it to be superior personally (Curtis, 2011).

THEORETICAL ORIENTATIONS

Psychoanalytic

Psychoanalytic groups help people attempt to understand and to gain insight about interactions with others, how groups affect individuals, and how to cope with the broader society and its institutions. It may be that in the process individuals come to realize how they are repeating interactional patterns and experiencing emotions that were important in the past and thus develop new ways of coping.

Obviously interpretation and the examination of dreams are important in psychoanalytic groups, but inquiry has been a major form of therapeutic intervention at least since the time of Sullivan (1953).

Traditional psychoanalytic concepts such as analyzing transference, valuing unconscious processes and analyzing resistance had to be altered to some extent when applied to groups as opposed to the original two-person situation. Transferences, and co-transferences, developed among group members, not simply toward the leader and vice versa. Processes occurred that often appeared to be out of the awareness of group members, but were not simply intrapsychic within the minds of individuals, but at a group level. Many of these processes had been anticipated by Freud in his *Group Psychology and the Analysis of the Ego* and in *Totem and Taboo*, but others were articulated by

Bion (1961). Bion noticed three ways that groups often cope with anxiety, by dependency on the leader, by forming pairs, and by fight and flight. They often hope for a group savior and they often have issues with authority. In psychoanalytic group psychotherapy the therapist is usually more of a facilitator as opposed to someone conducting individual therapy in front of a group. In “group analysis,” there is an attempt to understand the person’s suffering in terms of the broader social issues, not simply as an intrapsychic process. Jungian analysts might lead participants in a guided fantasy such as imagining going up, as on a mountain, or down, as into the earth in order to aid the fantasy lives of people and expand their awareness. From a stages of change perspective (Prochaska and DiClemente, 2002), this type of group is well-suited when people are exploring the nature of their problems and deciding if they wish to undergo the costs and disadvantages of change, as well as the advantages.

Outcome research in psychoanalytic group therapy was conducted as early as 1975. Dick (1975) conducted a prospective study with neurotic and borderline patients (N = 93) spanning two years in which participants participated in closed psychodynamic therapy groups. All individuals completed assessments before, after, and at 6-, 18-, and 30-month post-baseline time points regarding life acceptability of sex, work, physical health, leisure, self-image, self-understanding, and symptoms. While a quarter of participants did not complete the study, a majority of those who did demonstrated positive change. Many of these participants were not receiving psychiatric services at the time.

Analytic group therapy efficacy studies have shown various results. Sharpe, Selley, Low, and Hall (2001) conducted a prospective study with male survivors of childhood sexual abuse (N = 27). Participants were recruited from a psychological therapy service to a slow-open group for 28 weeks, meeting weekly for an hour and a half. All participants completed the Beck Depression Inventory and the Spielberger State Anxiety Scale at pre-test, post-test, and six months follow-up. Researchers concluded that their slow-open men's group characterized as time-limited and single-sex provided a therapeutic environment that resulted in improvement, similar to previous literature on women's analytic group therapy. Overall, by the end of the 28-month treatment, participants experienced a significant decrease in depression and anxiety, but at the six-month follow-up, depression had increased for many.

Another prospective study examined the clinical effectiveness of patients in private practice (N = 69). Lorentzen, Bogwald, and Hoglend (2002) hypothesized that under "real life" clinical conditions, patients would change during group therapy on measures relating to psychological functioning, symptoms, and interpersonal problems. Furthermore, they anticipated that these changes would be maintained at a one-year follow-up. Participants were consecutively assigned to one of three treatment groups. All groups had the same male therapist but one group also was co-led by a female therapist. Participants varied in their Axis I and Axis II diagnoses, duration of problems, and GAF score. They spent an average of 32.5 months in analytic group therapy and improved significantly during therapy. At the one-year follow-up, more than half of participants had recovered or improved significantly. Researchers note that they had a very low number of dropouts, most likely because patients were carefully prepared prior to the study. Expectations were toned down and patients had to agree to participate for at six months. Only two participants did not complete the six-month minimum requirement. While researchers did conduct an uncontrolled study, the different therapists and diversity of patients allow these results to be generalized to other patients in private practice.

Difficulties in conducting randomized controlled trials of analytic group therapy and the conflicting results that are constantly discussed might have deterred many researchers from adding to the literature. Blackmore, Tantam, Parry, and Chambers (2011) conducted a systematic review of the efficacy and clinical effectiveness of group analysis and analytic/dynamic group psychotherapy. Of the 34 studies and 19 reviews researchers examined, very few were of high quality in regard to randomization and control, had inconsistent reporting, lacked defining terminology, and used poor key words in titles and abstracts.

Cognitive-Behavioral

Cognitive-behavioral groups focus on skills and problem-solving. Practicing new behaviors, role-playing, cognitive reframing, goal setting, and facilitating feedback from other participants are major parts of the process. The group therapist is directive and makes suggestions. From a stages of change perspective (Prochaska and DiClemente, 2002), this type of therapy is well-suited when individuals already know what they wish to change. It is often used with behavioral problems such as eating disorders, substance abuse, sexual behaviors such as exhibitionism, and lack of assertiveness. The Rational-Emotive therapy groups of Albert Ellis and his followers (Ellis and

Dryden, 1987) also fall into the broad range of cognitive-behavioral therapies and have similar principles.

Dialectical Behavior Therapy (Linehan, 1993) is often used for people who make suicidal gestures and have problems of destructive impulsive behaviors. This therapy is referred to as "Dialectical" because at the same time that the client is hoping to change, the client must also accept the way she or he is at the moment. Group skill training is an essential component of this therapy, in addition to the sessions with the therapist. The basic skills of Dialectical behavior therapy are mindfulness, distress tolerance, emotional regulation, and interpersonal effectiveness. Diaries are kept and life-threatening and treatment threatening behaviors are always addressed first.

Acceptance-Commitment Therapy was first implemented in the 1980's (Hayes et al., 2011). It emphasizes psychological flexibility and "contacting the present moment fully as a conscious human being" (www.contextual science.org/act). Group counseling sessions include didactic education as well as skills training, although this therapy is also offered individually. It attempts to help people engage in positive behaviors while experiencing difficult thoughts and feelings. Although similar conceptually in many ways to DBT, it also encourages perspective-taking on the self, the identification of values, and commitment to values. The word "training" is often used to avoid the stigma of the word "therapy."

Skills groups. A wised variety of skills training is provided for the chronically mentally ill and substance abusers. These groups may focus on budgeting money, activities of daily living, identifying feelings, ways of coping, etc. Often in these groups lists are handed out to participants to check off issues with which they are dealing or the items that apply to them most. These groups are led by mental health professionals.

Research support. Given that group therapy offers cost-effectiveness and a means of reducing isolation and loneliness common in old age, researchers have compared the treatment outcomes of CBT to that of psychodynamic group therapy. For example, Steuer et al. (1984) measured whether depressed geriatric patients would respond to group therapy and if so, which would be most effective. All participants who completed the nine-month treatment (N = 20) met the criteria for a DSM III diagnosis of major depressive disorder, were above the age of 55, and scored at least a 16 on the 21-item version of the Hamilton Depression Scale. Four groups, two with each type of treatment, were conducted and patients were assigned according to the time they entered the study. Measures included observer ratings on the Hamilton Depression Scale and the Hamilton Anxiety Scale, as well as self-ratings on the Zung Self-

Rating Depression Scale and the Beck Depression Inventory. Results indicated that patients in both cognitive-behavioral group therapy and psychodynamic group therapy demonstrated significant reductions on observer-rated measures of depression and anxiety and self-reported measures of depression. While there were no clinically significant differences between groups, the Beck Depression Inventory resulted in a statistically significant difference in favor of cognitive-behavioral treatment.

More recently, Echeburúa, Sarasua, and Zubizarreta (2014) examined the clinical effectiveness of CBT in a sample of battered women. Specifically, researchers were interested in whether individual therapy could be improved if supplemented with group therapy. Participants were volunteers from a mental health center in Alava, Spain (N = 116) who were being treating for symptoms related to male intimate partner violence, were not living with their abusive partner, and did not suffer from a severe psychological disorder. After an assessment phase, participants were consecutively assigned to one of two experimental groups: a combined treatment group of CBT on an individual and group basis and an individual treatment group of CBT on an individual basis. Variables relating to intimate partner violence and pathology were assessed at the assessment phase and at all post-baseline time points. A trained CBT psychotherapist conducted all individual and combined treatment sessions. Sessions focused on the treatment of post-traumatic stress disorder, emotional discomfort, and impaired functioning and addressed emotional expression, psychoeducation, trauma re-exposure, coping skills, and problem-solving. Results demonstrated that in comparison to individual CBT, participants in the combined treatment group had better outcomes when coping with post-traumatic stress disorder symptoms and with impaired functioning in everyday life. The effect size of the difference, however, was moderate. While group therapy as a supplement to individual CBT might be beneficial, researchers advise accommodating the needs of the battered women into the treatment plan to achieve the best outcomes.

The efficacy of dialectical behavior therapy (DBT) has been established for the overall improvement of symptomology of borderline personality disorder (BPD). Andión et al. (2012) examined this efficacy further by analyzing the reduction of suicide attempts, self-harm behaviors, visits to emergency departments, and dropout rates in BPD patients. Specifically, researchers hypothesized that a combined treatment of individual and group DBT would demonstrate a greater improvement on outcome measures, as well as dropout rates, in comparison to individual DBT. Participants were BPD outpatients admitted to a BPD treatment program (N = 51). Participants completed 12 months of the DBT therapy, attend an end-of-therapy interview, and attend an 18-month follow-up interview. In total, 40 participants completed the study. Results demonstrated a clinically significant change on all therapeutic outcome variables across both experimental groups. Similarly, a low dropout rate was seen during the administration of both types of DBT. Lastly, group dialectical behavioral therapy was not statistically significantly more effective than individual DBT. Researchers advise that given the costly resource requirements of group DBT, individual DBT will suffice in the treatment of BPD outpatients. In this study alone, individual DBT resulted in a decrease of 96 hours of therapeutic work without sacrificing reductions in the study's outcome variables.

Experiential and Systemic

Experiential groups have a number of theoretical orientations and histories, including those derived from the person-centered approach of Carl Rogers, the Gestalt theory of Fritz Perls., the experiential and emotional-narrative approaches of Leslie Greenberg and Lyn Angus, and existential theory, best known by the work of Irvin Yalom.

Rogerian (Rogers, 1970; 1961) or client-centered therapy is non-directive. The facilitator is emanate to unconditional positive regard for each person (not the behaviors) and to be authentic. Empathy is seen as the crucial mechanism of change. Rogers emphasized the discrepancy between the ideal self and the actual self as problematic, although this is considered to be the case in all therapies. Gestalt therapy groups (Perls, Hefferline and Goodman, 1951; Perls, 1969) empathize being in the "here and now," focusing on the senses instead of thoughts, the concept of "unfinished business," and the use of language that denies choice and power, such as phrases beginning with "I can't" and "it" or "you" instead of "i." In Gestalt groups one person may take the "hot seat" after volunteering to "work." Also used in Gestalt work is the "two chair" dialogues where a person switches chairs becoming the different parts of self that are in conflict or the self and another in conflict. Particularly useful is the Gestalt technique of asking a person to "become" in imagination the different people and objects in a dream and experience the self as these different entities. Such activity expands the ways of being. Greenberg combined the person-oriented and Gestalt approaches to form experiential groups (also called process-centered groups) and most recently has worked with Angus to combine his emotion-focused therapy with narrative therapies (Greenberg and Angus, 2011).

Perhaps the best known practitioner of group therapy is Irvin Yalom (Yalom and Leszcz, 2005; Yalom, 1970). Yalom comes from an existential theoretical background, emphasizing the role of choice in one's life. Yalom and Leszcz (2005) articulated the following main principles of group therapy: cohesiveness, universality, existential choices, altruism, installation of hope, recapitulating of primary family experiences, socializing techniques, interpersonal learning, imitation, catharsis, improving information, and self-understanding.

Systemic therapies are derived from family therapies. They also examine current relationship patterns and attempt to identify stagnant patterns regardless of the cause. The therapist tries to nudge the people in new directions. The approach is based upon cybernetics, where, as in the body, there are multiple forces acting at once that then affect one other.

Klontz, Wolf, and Bivens (2000) examined the effectiveness of a multimodal brief group experiential psychotherapy approach in participants with a variety of diagnoses (N = 41), including anxiety disorders, mood disorders, and an adjustment disorder. All participants were diagnosed by a licensed clinical psychologist according to the DSM-IV. Participants were invited by mail requesting their participation as volunteers. All participants were administered self-report instruments to assess for patterns of psychological symptomology, severity of depression, and self-actualization prior to, immediately after, and six months after the treatment. Participants took part in an eight-day residential group-experiential therapy treatment program involving 30 hours of intensive group experiential therapy with a focus on psychodrama. This included exercises in warm-up, action, and sharing phases. In addition to group therapy, participants spent six hours in activities designed to be metaphoric experiential teaching tools, such as wall-climbing or challenge course initiatives. Lastly, participants also attended psychoeducational seminars based on the therapeutic issues relating to this approach totaling 15 hours. Throughout the treatment program, mood-altering substances were discontinued for all participants. Results demonstrated effectiveness in reducing negative psychological symptoms, including fewer feelings of inadequacy, fewer irrational fear responses, and less paranoid behavior. These changes were stable at the six-month follow-up. Psychological well-being was also enhanced in instances including being more oriented to the present, more sensitive to person feelings and needs, and more able to see people as essentially good and synergic in understanding human nature. These changes were also stable at the six-month follow-up. While this study lacked controlled conditions that are central to efficacy studies, the foundation for utilizing this treatment approach is clearly established.

Person-centered group therapy has also been measured for degree of efficacy. Braaten (1989) examined the effects this modality has on a sample of mental health professionals, graduate students in clinical psychology, and normal graduate student controls (N = 111). These categories of participants resulted in two experimental groups and a control group. Three mental health professional groups and six graduate student groups met once a week for three-hour sessions over a period of 14 weeks. Variables of interest included positive goal attainment, symptom reduction, and group atmosphere and climate assessed at pre-test and post-test time points measured by the Therapy Project List-90, the Symptom Check List 90R, the Group Atmosphere Scale, and the Group Climate Questionnaire. Results indicated a significant improvements for mental health professionals but not for graduate students in relation to positive goal attainment. These findings were not held maintained for symptom reduction. Braaten (1989) explains that mental health professionals might have improved better than the graduate students because of the way they approached the study. They were more invested given they were paying a standard fee while students did not pay a fee and also received course credit. Person-centered group therapy was also related to significant increases in the group's atmosphere and climate. The researcher concludes that when working with a non-pathological sample, it is important to focus on positive gains and self-actualization, not just psychopathology, in order to see improvements.

Cho and Chen (2011) studied the effects of Gestalt group therapy on college students who experienced parental divorce in childhood in a sample of participants in southern Taiwan (N = 30). All participants were administered the Loss Inventory and the Chinese version of the Beck Depression Inventory at pre-test, post-test, and follow-up time points and were randomly assigned to one of two groups. The Gestalt experimental group received 18 hours of therapy over three days. Results demonstrated a general alleviation of participants' grief in the experimental group receiving Gestalt group therapy. Additionally, at follow-up, participants' friends, parents, and participants themselves reported positive changes in emotions, behaviors, thoughts, physiological conditions and interpersonal relations.

Szabó, Tóth, and Pakai (2014) tested the efficacy of a narrative group therapy method based on previous research using narrative psychological approaches for alcohol-dependent patients. Researchers hypothesized that by restructuring alcohol abuser's autobiographies in a controlled setting, patients will experience therapeutic effects and recovery. The study included an experimental group of patients treated at a rehabilitation ward with an admission diagnosis of alcohol dependence according to the ICD-10 (N = 30) and two control groups. The first control group differed from the experimental group in that they simply were not assigned to the autobiography reconstruction group and participated in other group therapies not discussed in the article. The second control group were patients being treated for unspecified anxiety disorders. All participants completed the Hopelessness Scale (HS) and the Means-Ends Problem Solving Procedure (MEPS) before and after the treatment phase of three weeks. During the autobiography reconstruction group sessions, participants completed four steps: writing autobiographies, sharing and discussing them with the group, writing new, guided autobiographies based on narrative psychology principles, and sharing and discussing the new autobiographies. Results of this preliminary study indicated a significant difference between the experimental and control groups. The narrative group therapy method appeared to reduce hopelessness and increased problem solving ability more effectively than the other group therapies. Limitations of this study should be considered, however. Researchers did not examine the long-term efficacy narrative group therapy might have in comparison to the control groups and did not discuss the other group therapies control group participants took part in. Generally, narrative group therapy appears to be effective for alcohol-dependent patients.

The efficacy of systemic group therapy has been measured against that of analytic group therapy in a sample of women with a history of child abuse. Elkjaer, Kristensen, Mortensen, Poulsen, and Lau (2014) examined the improvement of general symptomology, psychological functioning, and interpersonal problems in a randomized controlled trial involving a one-year follow-up. Participants were women randomly assigned to one of two experimental groups who completed pre-treatment, post-treatment, and one-year post-baseline assessments. Results indicted significant differences in improvement for both treatment modalities, but differences were significantly greater for systemic group therapy immediately after treatment. At the one-year follow-up, both modalities maintained significant improvements in treatment outcomes, but improvements were maintained for analytic group therapy while decreased for systemic group therapy. At this time, more than half of the participants experienced above the cut-off for caseness for general symptomology. While systemic group therapy appeared to be significantly more effective immediately after treatment, long-term follow-up did not indicate greater efficacy.

PERSONAL GROWTH AND SUPPORT GROUPS

As is obvious from the review of the history of group psychotherapy, the difference in the types of groups available for personal growth for people who have a psychiatric diagnosis and those who do not are not completely different. The Tavistock Clinic in London was involved in training leaders at least as far back as World War II and after that, Kurt Lewin advanced the notion of training groups in the United States. It remains unclear just what approaches are more effective for people with severe problems and those with the typical problems of everyday life, other than that most mental health professionals believe that it is more appropriate to give direct advice, suggestions, and structure to people with more serious problems. It is generally accepted that the almost complete lack of structure, such as that which exists in most Tavistock groups, is too anxiety-provoking for people who do not have clear sense of their own identity and good reality-testing (Sullivan, 1953). This type of group, however, was always intended for training leaders and understanding relationships among subgroups and relationship with authorities, not for persons with psychiatric disorders.

Training groups and sensitivity groups. These groups do not have a set agenda, but have values related to democracy and learning how to learn. The group leader is a facilitator helping participants to express their emotions and learn how they are coming across to others. The group emphasizes principles of good feedback, participant observation, unfreezing and uses cognitive aids. One such aid is called the Johari window of four cells where in one cell information is known to both self and others, in another, information is known neither to self or others, in one cell information is known to the self but not to others and, in the final cell, information is known to others but not to the self. One goal of the group is to increase the information known both to self and others. Structured exercises may be used, such as those published by Pfeiffer and Jones (1974).

The phrase "encounter group" has been used to include e a number of types of groups, including Esalen groups, marathon, sensory awareness, transactional analysis and psychodrama groups. Carl Rogers, as mentioned previously initiated work on encounter groups, using the phrase of Moreno. Much work followed by proponents such as Will Schutz (1973). These groups became popular at the Esalen Institute in Big Sur, California, in the 1960's and then elsewhere in the US. Some groups went on without sleep and were referred to as marathon groups. In the transactional analysis groups, people attempted to determine if their conversations were of the sort mother-child, etc. (Berne, 1964).

Extensive research on encounter groups and t-groups was published in a book by Lieberman, Yalom and Miles (1973). Of the 210 original participants, 170 completed the 30- hour training; over three months; 69 people served as a control group. They were given an extensive psychological battery before, at termination and six months after the training ended. According to the psychological batteries, of the 206 in the experimental group, 8% had a negative change at the end of the experience, whereas 23% in the control group did. For the experimental 38% were unchanged, with 60% in the control group, for the experimental 20% had moderate change with 13% in the control group. The results at the six-month follow-up were not very different. Of those who participated, 78% said it was constructive and 90% thought should be a regular elective in college. Yalom found that problems arose when leaders were overly provocative. Further research regarding the casualties in these groups (Kaplan, Obert, and Baskin, 1980) found that they were fewer than originally estimated and came from poor management of conflict.

The term *self-help group* cannot easily be interchanged with *support group*. Brabender, Fallon, and Smolar (2004) describe a support group as being routinized meeting of people with a common problem. These individuals either experience illness because of this problem or feel stigmatized. Support groups are often led by a professional with knowledge of treating the problem. A self-help group is also a routinized meeting of people brought together by a common problem, but is facilitated by group members themselves. Members make decisions regarding the setting, cost of help, and obtain resources for treatment.

Self-help groups have generally found support in research. For example, Lieberman (1993a) explains that self-help groups are particularly effective in regard to some aspects of bereavement while others, such as guilt or anger toward the deceased, are more effectively treated with psychotherapy. Lieberman suggests that irrational guilt or anger is best understood by unconscious conflicts, which typically does not have a place in a group therapy setting.

Alcoholics Anonymous (AA) offers support through a model of 12 steps. Ferri, Amato, and Davoli (2006) assessed the effectiveness of Twelve Step Facilitation (TSF) programs, primarily AA, compared to other interventions in reducing alcohol intake, achieving abstinence, maintaining abstinence, improving the quality of life of affected people and their families, and reducing alcohol associated accidents and health problems. Researchers conducted a search of trials from six databases. Eight trials were included involving adults of both genders with alcohol dependence attending on a voluntary or coerced basis, according to the inclusion and exclusion criteria. Researchers could not conclude that AA or any TSF program demonstrates effectiveness for reducing alcohol dependence or problems. They did find that AA may help patients remain in treatment more than alternatives but did differ in the amount of drinks and percentage of drinking days against other treatments. Researchers advise that more efficacy studies need to be conducted in order to make conclusive statements.

Others might argue that programs like AA are just as effective as other treatment programs in keeping people sober but studies rely solely on self-report questionnaires to analyze (Blonigen, Timko, Moos, and Moos, 2009; Gossop et al., 2003; Kelly, 2013; Kingree and Thompason, 2011;). Personality-based questionnaires are often, however, unreliable in predicting trends over time.

Gossop et al. (2003) avoided collecting data via self-report surveys in correlating attendance to AA meetings to outcomes. Participants were referred from a short-stay inpatient unit for the treatment and rehabilitation of alcoholism problems (N = 150). All participants had been diagnosed with alcohol dependence according to the ICD-10. They were interviewed shortly after being admitted to the unit and approximately five months after being discharged. A total of 120 participants completed the study. Variables of interest included frequency of AA attendance, quantity of drinks, and reported problems.

Results demonstrated that frequent AA visitors had superior drinking outcomes to non-AA visitors and infrequent visitors. While many participants still experienced psychiatric problems at follow-up, researchers advanced research in this field with their use of semi-structured interviews to collect data. Future research should rely on observable data in order to confirm efficacy of these programs.

Treatment for substance abuse focuses on either abstinence or reduction. CBT in groups has been found to be effective for substance abusers (Carrol et al., 1994; Rawson et al., 2002; Carrol, Rounsaville, and Gawin, 1996). For research on smoking cessation, please see Prochaska and DiClimente (2002). Smokenders (Smokenders.com) is an old and effective program using a wide variety of behavioral and other group methods.

CONCLUSION

Group treatments are likely here to stay. Work comparing the effectiveness of group treatments to that of individual treatments is still in its infancy, as is that of the entire field of psychotherapy research. There is little yet known about what sorts of treatment are most effective for what sort of people with particular problems. Overall, we know that psychotherapy appears to be effective (Seligman, 1995). Yalom and Leszcz (2005) ended their book with a caution to balance tradition with innovation, reminding one that evidence, not fashion, should determine what approaches are used. Dies (1994) concluded his extensive review of group therapies by noting that whereas structured therapies show more favorable outcomes (Dies, 1994), the preponderance of evidence shows no superiority of specific techniques or particular schools (Ahn and Wampold, 2001). In fact, what is most consistent in psychotherapy research is the finding that it is the relationship that is most important (Norcross, 2011). In groups, it may be the relationships among the participants, not the relationship with the facilitator, which are most important, although the facilitator obviously has something to do with the quality of the relationships that are formed.

REFERENCES

Ahn, H. and Wampold, B. E. (2001). Where oh where are the specific ingredients? A meta-analysis of component studies in counseling and psychotherapy. *Journal of Counseling Psychology*, 48(3), 251-257.

Andión, O., Ferrer, M., Matali, J., Gancedo, B., Calvo, N., Barral, C., … Torrubia, R. (2012). Effectiveness of combined individual and group dialectical behavior therapy compared to only individual dialectical behavior therapy: A preliminary study. *American Psychological Association,* 49(2), 241-250.

Berne, E. (1964). Games people play—The basic handbook of transactional analysis. New York: Ballantine Books.

Bion, W. R. (1961). Experiences in groups. London: Tavistock.

Blackmore, C., Tantam, D., Parry, G., and Chambers, E. (2011). Report on a systematic review of the efficacy and clinical effectiveness of group analysis and analytic/dynamic group psychotherapy. *Group Analysis,* 45(1), 46-69.

Blonigen, D. M., Timko, C., Moos, B. S., and Moos, R. H. (2009). Treatment, Alcoholics Anonymous, and 16-year changes in impulsivity and legal problems among men and women with alcohol use disorders. *Journal of Studies on Alcohol and Drugs,* 70(5), 714.

Braaten, L. J. (1989). The effects of person-centered group therapy. *Person-Centered Review,* 4(2), 183-209.

Brabender, V. A., Fallon, A. E., and Smolar, A. I. (2004). Essentials of group therapy. Hoboken, NJ: Wiley.

Brown, D. (1983). Dr S. H. Foulkes (1898–1976). *International Journal of Psycho-Analysis,* 64,109-109.

Carrol, K. M., Rounsaville, B. J., Nich, C., Gordon, L. T., Wirtz, P. W., Gawin, F. H. (1994). One-year follow-up of psychotherapy and pharmacotherapy for cocaine dependence: Delayed emergence of psychotherapy effects. *Archives of General Psychiatry*, 51, 989-997.

Carrol, K. M., Rounsaville, B. J., Gawin, F. H. (1996). A comparative trial of psychotherapies for ambulatory cocaine abusers. *American Journal of Drug and Alcohol Dependence,* 17, 229-247.

Cho, W. C., and Chen, C. S. (2011). The effects of Gestalt group therapy on college experiences parental divorced in childhood. *Chinese Journal of Guidance and Counseling,* 30, 69-100.

Curtis, R. C. (2011). Speaking freely: My experiences in individual psychotherapies, group psychotherapies, and growth groups. *Journal of Clinical Psychology: In Session.*

Dick, B. (1975). A ten-year study of out-patient analytic group therapy. *British Journal of Psychiatry,* 127, 365-375.

Dies, R. R. (1994). Therapist variables in group psychotherapy research. In A. Fuhriman and G. Burlingame (Eds.), Handbook of group psychotherapy (pp. 114-154). New York, NY: Wiley.

Dies, R. R. (2003). Group psychotherapies. In A. S. Gurman and S. B. Messer (Eds.) Essential Psychotherapies (pp. 515-550). New York Guilford.

Echeburúa, E., Sarasau, B., Zubizarreta, I. (2014). Individual versus individual and group therapy regarding a cognitive-behavioral treatment for battered women in a community setting. *Journal of Interpersonal Violence*, 29(10), 1783-1801.

Elkjaer, H., Kristensen, E., Mortensen, E. L., Poulsen, S., and Lau, M. (2014). Analytic versus systemic group therapy for women with a history of child sexual abuse: 1-year follow-up of a randomized controlled trial. *Psychology and Psychotherapy*, 87(2), 191-208.

Ellis, A., and Dryden, W. (1987). The practice of rational emotive therapy. New York, NY: Springer Publishing Company.

Ferri, M., Amato, L., and Davoli, M. (2006). Alcoholics anonymous and other 12-step programmes for alcohol dependence. The Cochrane Database of Systematic Reviews, (3).

Gossop, M., Harris, J., Best, D., Man, L. H., Manning, V., Marshall, J., and Strang, J. (2003). Is attendance at Alcoholics Anonymous meetings after inpatient treatment related to improved outcomes? A 6-month follow-up study. *Alcohol and Alcoholism*, 38(5), 421-426.

Greenberg, L. S., and Angus, L. E. (2011). Working with narrative in emotion-focused therapy: Changing stories, healing lives. Washington, DC: American Psychological Association.

Hayes, S. C., Stroshal, K. D., Wilson, K. G. (2011). Acceptance and commitment therapy: The process and practice of mindful change. (2nd ed.). New York, NY: Guilford Press.

Kaplan, R. E., Obert, S. L., and Van Buskirk, W. R. (1980). The etiology of encounter group casualties: Second facts. *Human Relations*, 33, 131-148.

Kelly, J. F. (2013). Alcoholics Anonymous science update: Introduction to the special issue. *Substance Abuse*, 34(1), 1-3.

Kingree, J. B., and Thompson, M. (2011). Participation in Alcoholics Anonymous and post treatment abstinence from alcohol and other drugs. *Addictive behaviors*, 36(8), 882-885.

Klontz, B. T., Wolf, E. M., and Bivens, A. (2000). The effectiveness of a multimodal brief group experiential psychotherapy approach. *International Journal of Action Methods,* 53(3/4), 119-135.

Lieberman, M. A. (1993a). A reexamination of adult life crises: Spousal loss in mid- and late life. In G. H. Pollock and S. I. Greenspan (Eds.), The course of life (pp. 69-110). Madison, CT: International Universities Press.

Lieberman, M. A., Yalom, I. D., Miles, M. B. (1973). Encounter groups: First facts. New York, NY: Basic Books.

Linehan, M. M. (1993). Cognitive behavioral treatment of borderline personality disorder. New York, NY: Guilford Press.

Lorentzen S., Bogwald, K., and Hoglend, P. (2002). Change during and after long-term analytic group psychotherapy. *International Journal of Group Psychotherapy*, 52(3), 419-429.

Norcross, J. C. (2011). Psychotherapy relations that work: Evidence-based responsiveness. New York, NY: Oxford University Press.

Perls, F. S. (1969). Gestalt therapy verbatim. Boulder, CO: Real People Press.

Perls, F. S., Hefferline, R., and Goodman, P. (1951). Gestalt therapy: Excitement and growth in the human personality. New York, NY: Julian Press.

Pertegato, E. G. and Pertegato, G. O. (2013). From psychoanalysis to group analysis. London: Karnac.

Pfeiffer, J. W. and Jones, J. E. (1974). Structured experiences for human relations training. San Diego: University Associates.

Prochaska, J., and DiClemente, C. (1983). Stages and processes of self-change of smoking: Toward an integrative model of change. *Journal of Consulting and Clinical Psychology,* 51(3), 390-395.

Prochaska, J. O., and DiClimente, C. C. (2002). Transtheoretical therapy. In J. Lebow (Ed.), Comprehensive handbook of psychotherapy, Vol. 4, Integrative-eclectic (pp. 165-184). New York: Wiley.

Prochnik, G. (2006). Putnam Camp: Sigmund Freud, James Jackson Putnam, and the purpose of American psychology. New York, NY: Other Press.

Rawson, R. A., Huber, A., McCann, M. J., Shoptaw, S., Farabee, D., Reiber, C. … Ling, W. (2002). A comparison of contingency management and cognitive-behavioral approaches during methadone maintenance for cocaine dependence. *Archives of General Psychiatry*, 59, 817-824.

Rogers, C. R. (1961). On becoming a person; a therapist's view of psychotherapy. Boston, MA: Houghton Mifflin.

Rogers, C. R. (1970). Carl Rogers on encounter groups. New York, NY: Harper and Row.

Scheidlinger, S. (1992). On adolescent violence: Some preliminary group process observations. Unpublished manuscript, Albert Einstein College of Medicine, Brooklyn, NY.

Schutz, W. C. (1973). Elements of encounter. New York, NY: Irvington Publishers.

Seligman, M. E. (1995). The effectiveness of psychotherapy: The consumer reports study. *The American Psychologist*, 50(1), 965-974.

Sharpe, J., Selley, C., Low, L., and Hall, Z. (2001). Group analytic therapy for male survivors of childhood sexual abuse. *Group Analysis*, 34(2), 195-209.

Steuer, J. L., Mintz, J., Hammen, C. L., Hill, M. A., Jarvik, L. F., McCarley, T., Motoike, P., and Rosen, R. (1984). Cognitive-behavioral and psychodynamic group psychotherapy in treatment of geriatric depression. *Journal of Consulting and Clinical Psychology*, 52(2), 180-189.

Sullivan, H. S. (1953). The interpersonal theory of psychiatry. New York, NY: Norton.

Szabó, J., Tóth, S., and Pakai, A. K. (2014). Narrative group therapy for alcohol dependent patients. *International Journal of Mental Health and Addictions,* 12.

Welcome to SmokEnders. (n.d.). Welcome to SmokEnders. Retrieved July 31, 2014, from http://www.smokenders.com/index.htm

Yalom, I. D., and Leszcz, M. (2005). The theory and practice of group psychotherapy, 5th ed. New York, NY: Basic Books.

Yalom, I. D. (1970). The theory and practice of group psychotherapy. New York, NY: Basic Books.

In: Group Therapy
Editor: Hellen Derrickson

ISBN: 978-1-63463-173-0

Chapter 3

GROUP DYNAMICS IN OLDER PEOPLE'S CLOSED GROUPS: FINDINGS FROM FINNISH PSYCHOSOCIAL GROUP REHABILITATION FOR LONELY OLDER PEOPLE

Kaisu H. Pitkälä*, Niina Savikko and Pirkko Routasalo
University of Helsinki, Department of General Practice and Primary Health Care and Helsinki University Central Hospital, Unit of Primary Health Care, Finland

ABSTRACT

Our qualitative study explores the dynamics, phenomena, and processes occurring in 12 older people's closed groups, which were arranged as a psychosocial group intervention for older adults suffering from loneliness. The groups were formed to alleviate loneliness. We aimed to reduce the heterogeneity of participants during recruitment. Individuals with significant dementia, mobility disability, or sensory deficits were therefore excluded. The group programs were arranged according to participant interests so as to ensure that individuals with

* Correspondence to: Kaisu H Pitkälä, MD, PhD, professor. University of Helsinki, Department of General Practice and Primary Health Care, PO Box 20, 00014 University of Helsinki, tel. +358-50-3385546; fax. +358-9-1911 27536; email: kaisu.pitkala@helsinki.fi.

similar interests would be grouped together (art, exercise). All groups included 7–8 participants (N=93; females n=68, mean age 80) and they met once a week on 12 occasions (6 hours/day) during three months. All groups had two professional group facilitators.

We used three different types of data and grounded theory to explore the occurring group processes: 1) facilitators' detailed descriptions from each group meeting (ca. 300 pages); 2) researchers' observations and field notes of group visits (two/each group); 3) participants' feedback of the groups.

Each group went through a common path from one stage to another: from initial chaos to an effectively working and self-directed group. The entire life course was experienced by 11/12 groups, although differences were observed in development speed. Other special characteristics were detected in the lonely older people's groups. Some are features typical of all older people's groups (diseases, heterogenic functional status), and some are probably typical for only these types of loneliness groups (difficulties in adhering to their group, reluctance to discuss feelings of loneliness), art groups (courage to try new things with peer support, avoiding conversations about diseases), exercise groups (eroticism, competition between group members), and some phenomena might be specific for several group types (flirting, a common secret between group members, a common enemy increasing group cohesion). Participants had some common group roles in these groups (e.g. leader, critic, silent, dominant, team spirit creator, disabled).

Group dynamics and group roles in older people's groups resemble those known from adult groups. However, some features are different and could be taken into account when planning and gathering therapeutic groups for older people.

INTRODUCTION

Support groups and group therapy have been used for decades in older people's care and rehabilitation (Burnside & Schmidt 1994). Group therapy is a well-established treatment modality for depressed or socially isolated older adults (Schulman 1985, Gorey & Cryns 1991, Clark & Vorst 1994, Husaini et al. 2004, Agronin 2009). Support groups for relatives, caregivers, or widows are examples of psychosocial group treatments (Toseland et al. 1989, Marriott et al. 2000, Stewart et al. 2001). A variety of group types exist for older people, ranging from activity groups to more specific psychodynamic groups (Agronin 2009). Older people's group therapy has been shown to be effective in helping older adults. The effect sizes of group therapy are moderate to large according to a meta-analysis by Payne & Marcus (2008).

Group dynamics and processes have been studied in adult groups as early as the 1940s by Foulkes, Bion or Levin (Ettin et al. 1997). In older people's groups, however, the variance and significance of group processes has not received much attention (Toseland 1990, Burnside & Schmidt 1994, Lavoie 1995, Agronin 2009) and group dynamics research has been scarce (Schmidt & Keyes 1985, Evans et al. 2001, Saiger et al. 2001, Perraud et al. 2004, Christensen et al. 2006, Toseland and Rivas 2005). To our knowledge, some studies have explored specific aspects of group dynamics in older people's groups, e.g. how participants' male gender impacts the dominance of group discussions (de Medeiros et al. 2007) or how the active roles of group leaders may impact a group's tempo (Weiner and Weinstock 1979–80). However, comprehensive investigations on group dynamics are lacking.

We conducted a randomized controlled trial in 2003–2005 on lonely older people aiming to alleviate their loneliness, empower them, support their self-efficacy, and enable peer support in the groups (Savikko et al. 2010). We were able to show that this group intervention improved older people's quality of life (QOL), cognition and health, enhanced their new friendships, and decreased their use of health and social services and mortality (Pitkala et al. 2009, Routasalo et al. 2009, Pitkala et al. 2011). Our article is based on a qualitative study, which explores the dynamics and developmental process of 12 intervention groups of older adults during the course of three months.

CONTEXT

Older people are prone to feeling lonely. Losses, work retirement, the deaths of spouses and friends, and illnesses and disabilities lead to decreased social integrity (Routasalo & Pitkala 2003). Loneliness is associated with several adverse outcomes such as impaired QOL, cognitive decline, poor health, disabilities, increased use of health and social services, and increased mortality (Tilvis et al. 2000, Routasalo & Pitkala 2003).

Group Intervention Principles

We thus wished to examine whether psychosocial groups designed especially for lonely older people could reverse these adverse effects. We recruited 235 participants with the aid of a national survey exploring older people's (75+) loneliness, social relationships, recreational activities, and interests (Routasalo et al. 2006, Tilvis et al. 2011). Respondents stating that they suffer from loneliness were randomized into two arms: an intervention group receiving psychosocial group rehabilitation and a control group. We used the stratified randomization procedure in the following way: participants stating similar interests (exercise, art, therapeutic writing) were randomized in groups of 16 (with eight participants entering intervention and eight functioning as the control). In this article we describe our findings from the art and exercise groups, which consisted of a total of 93 participants (mean age 80 years, age range 75 to 92 years).

A total of 12 lonely older people's groups were formed in 2003–2004, each consisting of 7–8 participants. Each group had 12 sessions during three months, meeting once a week for 5–6 hours at a time. These groups were arranged in six localities in Finland: in five communities and six rehabilitation centres for World War II veterans. The groups were closed and their composition remained the same during their whole life course. New members were not recruited if an individual did not attend or dropped out. We wished participants to feel safe, to attach and make friends with each other to alleviate their loneliness. Toseland & Rivas (2005) have stated that groups with frequent membership changes remain at the formative stage.

Group meetings were objective-oriented and group facilitators planned a program that participants were encouraged to modify. The participants were transported to group meetings and back by minibus. The meetings included coffee breaks and lunches. Everything was free of charge for the participants.

Irrespective of group content, the principles of psychosocial group rehabilitation intervention were the same in all groups. The professional group facilitators enhanced security and equal communication in the groups. They aimed to promote interaction and friendships between participants. Professionals worked more as facilitators than as active leaders. However, they worked actively to empower participants, enhanced their active participation, and stimulated their self-efficacy and problem-solving skills in line with self-management principles (Barlow et al. 2002, Bodenheimer 2002). We hypothesized that group dynamics will occur within the groups and members will experience the ups and downs of newly developing human relationships.

The group intervention aimed to enable participants to share their experiences with peers, discuss their feelings of loneliness, receive support, and develop feelings of solidarity. Details of the intervention have been described in another article (Savikko et al. 2010).

Group facilitators were professionals in older people's work: nurses, physiotherapists, and occupational therapists. When recruiting these professionals we wished to ensure that they value older people, are able to reflect on their work as group facilitators, and receive feedback for their work. Each group had two professional facilitators who received thorough training (Pitkala et al. 2004). Group facilitators additionally received work supervision during the entire group functioning period. Each facilitator pair coached two groups. The latter began when the first one finished.

Table 1. Characteristics of participants in the art and exercise groups

Characteristic	Art groups (N=47)	Exercise groups (N=46)
Mean age (range)	80 (75 – 91)	80 (76 to 92)
Females, n (%)	35 (75)	33 (72)
Lives alone, n (%)	39 (82)	37 (80)
Education <8 years, n (%)	31 (66)	28 (60)
MMSE[1], mean (range)	27.2 (21 to 30)	25.7 (19 to 30)
Often feels depressed, n (%)	8 (16)	2 (4)

[1] Minimental State Examination (Folstein et al. 1975).

PARTICIPANTS

We recruited participants with specific inclusion criteria. We wished to ensure that groups were fairly homogenous and participants had similar interests. All participants had stated that they suffer from loneliness. They had also indicated similar hobbies or interests in the survey, and the frame and contents of the group program were organized accordingly in each group. The randomization was performed in groups of 16 individuals with similar interests. Prior to randomization we thoroughly assessed all participants using cognitive and functional tests and excluded people with moderate or severe dementia. All participants had to be able to move independently with or without mobility devices. All had to see and hear sufficiently to be able to participate in the group work. By interviewing potential participants beforehand and using these inclusion and exclusion criteria we wished to ensure the homogeneity of the intervention groups (Agronin 2009). Participant characteristics are presented in Table 1. All groups had 2–4 males.

Group Activities and Contents

Participants with an interest in art and inspiring activities were placed in their own groups, whereas those with an interest in exercise formed their own groups. Various artists (musicians, actors, artists) attended the meetings of the art groups, the participants visited cultural events and sights and also actively produced their own art. Participants in the exercise groups performed various athletic tasks, e.g. Nordic stick walking, strength training, swimming, or senior dancing. We additionally arranged several hours for discussions in the groups during each session. All activities were adjusted according to the participants' physical condition and wishes.

The different group contents were consciously arranged in the intervention to be certain of captivating the attention of elderly people with various interests, so as to get them to commit themselves to the groups. The common interests of the groups also ensured that participants could find kindred spirit and potential friendships within the groups. Each group was planned so openly that group members always had the opportunity to influence the meeting programs.

Data Collection

Our study explores data from multiple sources.

The group facilitators wrote a diary entry of each group meeting. This material (ca. 300 pages) is abundant and consists of both descriptions of what happened in the groups as well as how participants behaved in the groups. Facilitators described the contents, events, participants' behavior, and interactions in the groups as well as reflectively considering the facilitators' own role and feelings of the events and interactions occurring in the groups. These diaries form the primary data used in our qualitative study investigating group phenomenon and dynamics. The authors (KHP, PR) additionally observed each group twice during their course. Field notes were written and also used as data material in our study.

We have additional data from the initial survey responses of each participant (Routasalo et al. 2006), concerning their feelings of loneliness, social networks, interests and preferences, as well as the study nurses' interviews and data measured on various scales concerning participants' functioning, cognition, QOL, depression, and health (Pitkala et al. 2009). We thus know whether participants had any sensory or cognitive problems or suffered from depression. Participants furthermore gave written half-structured feedback on their experiences of the group intervention. We thus have several data resources that may reinforce or contradict the hypothesis and ideas formulated from the primary data.

We use grounded theory as the basis of our qualitative analysis (Martin & Turner 1986). The diaries and field notes were analyzed using an inductive approach. The diaries were read several times: the first time when the researchers received them by e-mail after each group meeting. On the second time they were analyzed during work supervision sessions. When the diaries were read for the third time, they were coded using the NVIVO analysis program. The diaries were independently coded by three researchers.

Different occurrences and features that appeared in the diaries were coded into themes at the beginning of the analysis. These themes were next combined into categories. In the last phase the appearance of different phenomenon were tabulated to clarify their prevalence and absence in different groups as well as for deviating cases. Tabulation was additionally used because we wished to explore the possible differences between groups in relation to the appearance of a specific phenomenon on a time line.

We use citations to support and illustrate our findings and interpretations. Only short passages of the citations are presented, and the possibility of recognizing individual participants from them is obliterated.

Our study received permission from the local ethics committee. It was performed according to the Helsinki declaration. Each participant provided informed consent.

Developmental Stages of Older People's Groups

A common life course can be detected in all older people's groups, and this can be described by similar developmental stages in all groups. The developmental stages are introduced in Table 2.

Table 2. The development of the stages in older people's groups during their three-month course. Each group is described using a number. By following each number the development of a particular group from one stage to another (rows) can be observed in relation to the meetings (columns)

Group stage	1.session	2.session	3.session	4.session	5.session	6.session	7.session	8.session	9.session	10.session	11.session	12.session
At onset: chaos & role searching	1,2,3,4,5,6, 7,8,9,10,11,12	3, 9,11	3, 9,11	7			12					
Group formation	1,4,5,6, 10	1,2,3, 7,9,12	2,6, 7,8,9	7,9, 11	11	11						
"Honeymoon" – finding the team spirit		1,2,4,5,6 10	1,2,3,4,5,6,7,9,10,12	1,2,3,4, 7,8,9,10,12	3,4 7,9,10	3,4 7,8,9,10	7,8,11	7,9,		12		12
Trust and encouragement		4,5 10	1,5 7,8,9,10	1,2,6 7,9	1,3, 9	3,4, 9	3,4, 11	11				
Critics and conflicts		12	2,3,5, 12	1,3,5,6, 8,10,12	1,2,3,6, 7,10	1,3,4,6, 8,10,11,12	1,2,3,5,6, 7,8,9,11,12	3,4, 9,11	1,2, 7,11	3 4,5	1	
(Becoming tired)							3					
Effectively working group			5	2,4,5	1,2,5,6, 10	2,4,5,6, 8	1,2,4,5,6, 7,8,11	1,2,3,5,6, 7,10,11	2,3,5,6, 8	4,5, 7,8,10,11	3,5, 7,11	
Self-directed group				5	5	2,6	1,2,6, 7,10	1,2,3,5,6 9,11	4,5, 8,9,10	2,6, 7,9,10,11	1,2,3,4, 6,7	1,3,4
Mourning, future plans						1	2,4	1, 7	10	3,5,6, 7,8	2,3,4,5, 7,9,10,11	1,3,4,5,6, 7,8,9,10,11,12

The life and development of the groups advanced from one stage to another, and in a few cases a group returned to the previous stages to later advance once more. Not all groups went through every single stage (groups 9 and 12) but in general the groups matured step by step, learned to be efficient and active, became self-directed, mourned, and left farewells to the group. There were differences in developmental speed, but as a thumb rule these groups advanced quite fast to the effectively working and self-directed group stage (Table 2). Group development stages have been described in earlier literature, although fewer developmental stages have been described (Tuckman 1965, Luft 1970, Burnside & Schmidt 1994, Lenneer-Axelson & Thylefors 1998). To our knowledge, such explorations on older people's groups have not been performed before.

We give examples of these stages using extractions from the group facilitators' diaries.

Chaos, Searching for Roles

The participants' need for talking was evident in each group right from the beginning. In fact, several group facilitators wondered in their diaries whether such talkative older people can suffer from loneliness.

> "Speech babble filled the room… I began to wonder whether these people really needed this kind of group."

Contrary to our findings, the first meetings of some earlier studies of older people's groups have been described as exceptionally quiet (Burnside & Schmidt 1994). Some participants in three groups were a little tense and reserved, which the group leaders commented on in their diaries. Excitement concerning new things was noted.

Although all facilitators had instructed the groups with common ground rules (group organization consisting of the same people for 12 weeks, secrecy of other participant's issues outside the groups, respecting other participants, listening to others, avoiding interrupting others, speaking clearly) at the beginning, all groups had difficulties in forming safe group constructions and listening to others.

> "The day was a hodge-podge."

In several groups one participant expressed that she/he had expected to receive physical rehabilitation when coming to a rehabilitation center. In one group, one participant disappeared for a short time at the beginning. When dividing members into subgroups for participating in the joint activities, some participants had difficulties in collaborating. Mild power struggles were additionally detected during the first meeting. This occurred because some participants desired to take the position of leader, attract the facilitator's attention, or influence them.

> "Several people did their own thing instead of working as a group, and some got lost from the subject instead of cooperating."

The problems described above are typical for the initial stage of a group, which have been described by many authors (Tuckman 1965, Lenneer-Axelson & Thylefors 1994), although they have not often been explored in older people's groups.

Resistance to and testing of the group was additionally detected at the initial stage. During the first session one participant stated that he came to the group to see "*if there was any point in attending this group*".

> "Immediately after coming in B. remarked that he wouldn't have come if he would have known that he is the only man in the group."

Several groups had one participant who immediately blurted our "I am not lonely". Tuckman argued that hesitant participation is often observed at the initial stage, where members test the group and its leaders to discover how they will respond to various statements (Tuckman 1965).

All groups began with this initial "chaos, searching for roles" -stage. Three groups continued being chaotic for three sessions, whereas others progressed to the next stage, some even during the first session. Two groups had features of this initial stage even after developing to the next stages, thus returning momentarily to the chaotic phase.

Forming a Group

Member attachment and grouping was detected in the groups very early on, with several groups even exhibiting these traits during the first session, but mostly during the second or third session. Participants gave positive, polite feedback to the group facilitators and praised the group, as also described in previous literature (Lenneer-Axelson & Thylefors 1998). Participants expressed positive things to each other and avoided conflicts. The expression of one's own feelings was still exiguous at this point.

"C. said: ...wonderful, now I have one reason to leave home."

It appears that group facilitators opening up a discussion concerning loneliness had a catalytic effect on the forming stage. Some facilitators did not dare do this until the second or third session, which seemed to prolong the initial chaotic stage. All group facilitators discussed the problem of loneliness at their supervision sessions with us, and admitted that it is a challenging topic to bring up in the groups. They felt that it is a delicate matter, and a potential stigma on the participants.

The Honeymoon – Finding Our Team Spirit

Team spirit was observed at quite an early stage in each group. This emerged as participants found their own roles and the easiness of participating in the group. Each group developed its own humor typical to that particular group. A number of positive expressions of feelings were expressed towards other members (Burnside & Schmidt 1994, Lenneer-Axelson & Thylefors 1998). The honeymoon stage was obvious in most groups during the second or third session.

"Participants encouraged and praised each other when painting."
"The women talked about "our boys", noticed them to be an invaluable part of the group."

The participants began feeling attached to their own group. They began building subgroups, in which participants whispered with each other. Mutual assistance and support was also observed.

"G. and F. talked a lot with each other… U. and O. laughed with each other."

Subgroup development has earlier been considered as a threat for older people's groups (Burnside & Schmidt 1994), but it seemed to act as a promoter of mutual interaction in our groups.

Trust and Encouragement

When trust began growing between the participants they began expressing their sorrows and opening up to each other in a more courageous way than earlier. The group strongly supported those who expressed their woes.

> "X. expressed how hard it was when her child died at an early age, and she mentioned that her family will not continue anymore."
>
> "But the participants also received many words of consolation from each other."

At this stage the group was perceived as safe enough and participants had the courage to show their emotions, especially around art experiences. Music brought up some old memories, text reading inspired discussion concerning loneliness, or a movie encouraged to reflect one's own life course.

> ".., now she could tell us the reasons for her tears during the last session. … She expressed that her husband had played several instruments. ... Now she had her dead husbands' silent violin on the wall…"

Critics and Conflicts

Participants also dared to express criticism and anger towards the facilitators and the group, as they gradually became more acquainted with each other and their confidence grew. At this stage some insurgency could be observed in several groups. Participants resisted some group tasks and tested both the group facilitators and the group rules.

> "Participants said they cannot paint (group activity in an art group on that particular day), they don't have the courage to attend meetings anymore because tasks are too difficult…"

Earlier literature has argued that complaints and criticism are slight and concealed in older people's groups (Burnside & Schmidt 1994). We could interpret this to be the case also in our groups as criticism was often expressed using humor.

Mild disagreements also developed between participants in some groups at this stage, and they gave snappy feedback to each other.

> "G. noticed that she/he might be the only World War II refugee. Y. became provoked by this and remarked that you are not a refugee anymore."
>
> While participants painted new ties and scarves for themselves, once facilitator notes: "then T. wished to use the color orange to place his mark on the tie. S. remarked "you will not use that color!" and T. kept still for a while. Then T. took the paintbrush and painted a large orange ball on the tie tip. S. shouted in a very loud voice and concurrently trampled her foot: No! Now it is ruined."

However, conflicts between participants were relatively rare and mild. For example, participants were rather reluctant to give feedback to a dominant, talkative member.

> "K. told his own rambling stories while completely interrupting the others' talk. The participants tolerated and understood him."

Participants appeared to presume that facilitators would calm down a dominant member. It has been argued that groups have strong social control and the ability to recover its own actions (Lenneer-Axelson & Thylefors 1998). However, older people do not easily confront talkative, dominant group members. The politeness and modesty of this generation and difficulty to demand their own space has also been noted in previous studies (Bowers et al. 2001, Laakkonen et al. 2004).

A disturbing use of cell phones created discussion in one group. Several participants had cell phones with them and handled their own businesses in the middle of the group program. It has been noticed that insurgency and aggressive behavior are more unlikely in older people's groups than in groups with younger people (Toseland 1990). However, our data demonstrate that this is possible, although the insurgency and aggressiveness were mild.

Becoming Tired

The stage of "becoming tired", shown in previous studies among younger adults (Lenneer-Axelson & Thylefors 1998), was detected in only one group. This happened halfway through the group meetings during a session when this group had lived through the conflict stage. During that meeting the group criticized the previous weeks' program, and after this it was passive and surprisingly quiet for the rest of the meeting. Participants discussed their plans outside the group and some of them doubted their possibilities of participating in group meetings in the future. The participants were suddenly less committed to the group than before.

> "At the end of the day I felt somewhat flaked out. Feels like the group is somehow falling apart in different directions at this stage."

Effectively Working Group

Tranquillity took over in each group after the conflict phase. Participants adapted to the common rules and there was democracy in decision-making and balance in how everybody could take part in the discussions.

Conversations deepened. At this stage participants trusted each other. They had courage to try many surprising things, such as writing poems, theater improvisation, and expressing feelings through dance. Some participants seemed to surpass their own limits with the support of the group.

> "And then the series of ventures emerged and everyone received applauses after their own performance."

Participants appeared proud of their courage and what they had accomplished. Some wished to be photographed.

> "...so my grandchildren can see how their grandpa paints".

The Self-directed Group

The groups seemed to become independent and more self-directed in the middle or end of the groups' life course. Participants gradually took more initiative in suggesting the group program. They introduced their ideas to the group. Presents, such as home-made cakes, were common. In a few groups, a participant invited the group to visit their home. In one group, the participants proudly took the guidance of an excursion into their own hands and acted as local guides for the group.

Participants of five groups took the initiative of suggesting to continue group meetings on their own after the official part was over. Participants spontaneously changed telephone numbers and arranged meetings. They had their "own things" and laughed a lot during the breaks and lunch, when the group facilitators were not there. In several groups one person took the role of a leader. That person e.g. organized gifts for the facilitators and future meetings. Participants began acting as a group without the official leaders present.

> "Sometimes H. gave ...brisk instructions and said that it is "good we have a boss around here, as our real bosses are so quiet."

Mourning and Future Plans as the Final Group Stage

The ending of the group was discussed in each group. Sadness and grief was expressed.

> "R. was particularly quiet and serious. The end of the group work seemed to be very sad to her. She mentioned that several times during the day."

With some groups, discussions concerning group ending actually already began during the middle of the groups' life course. Some group members expressed their concern about the ending of the group meetings. The wish for "failing the course" was expressed by two groups, so they could continue for another 12 times.

Each group held a party on the last meeting. The participants bought flowers or other gifts to the group facilitators and gave speeches. The party and program was organized independently by the participants.

> "O. wanted to read a self-made thank you speech for us. He ended up crying during the first sentences."
>
> "They then appeared with flowers and handed them and a card over to us [the facilitators]..."

A couple of members in two groups, who had so far participated in every meeting, did not attend the last one. In addition, one participant of one group left for home in the middle of the last meeting. Goodbyes can be an overwhelmingly difficult situation for some people (Perraud et al. 2004), which might remind them of earlier experiences of abandonment experienced by these lonely older people.

How Can Understanding of Developmental Stages Be Used in Work with Older People?

The group facilitators' diaries used in our study are detailed step-by-step descriptions of the events that occurred in the groups. These findings could be confirmed by our own observations in groups. This enabled a systematic and detailed investigation and interpretation of the group dynamics in older people's groups. The developmental stages of the groups could be surprisingly clearly observed and they were similar to those discussed in previous literature (Tuckman 1965, Luft 1970, Burnside & Schmidt 1994, Lenneer-Axelson & Thylefors 1998). The stages of closed groups have been described in classical studies, e.g. in Bion's groups (Bion 2000), the forming-norming-storming-performing phenomenon (Tuckman 1965), or in the group life courses described by Lenneer-Axelson (Lenneer-Axelson & Thylerfors 1998). The "becoming tired" –stage as described by Lenneer-Axelson and Thylefors (1998) was observed in only one of our groups.

Two stages could be observed as novel and distinct in older people's group life courses. These stages might be special to lonely older people's groups. The first was "trust and encouragement", in which participants began expressing negative emotions and sorrows along with their positive feelings. These individuals suffered from loneliness. They may have experienced disappointments in their earlier life. Most had suffered losses. They may thus have been reserved and reluctant to express themselves and take risks in new relationships. In our groups they met peers with similar experiences, and possibly for this reason there was a clear stage during which — concurrently — everybody began opening up to each other. The other phase was the "self-directed group", during which the group began taking more responsibility of themselves as a group and of the group program. The aim of our intervention was to empower participants, and the facilitators worked towards this aim so that the groups would become self-directed and would continue meeting on their own. Gaining independence was a desired phenomenon in our groups. This stage may not necessarily exist in all elderly groups.

The development of a group through its different stages creates requirements and tools for group facilitators. The recognition of different stages helps facilitators be patient, guide the groups through the initial chaos, and also appreciate any conflicts, knowing that they are natural stages in group development. During the initial chaotic stage the group facilitator should clearly state the objectives and rules of the group, so that participants feel secure and adhere to the common task (Toseland 1990, Cockman et al. 1992). A common task and objective are essential for these groups, as without a common objective participants do not adhere to the groups' function (Toseland 1990, Burnside & Schmidt 1994). A common basic task describes why the group exists in the first place (Bion 2000, Cockman et al. 1992). The participants may have different views concerning this basic task, as was seen during the first meetings of our groups when some participants reported not feeling lonely. In this way they tried to step back and tell other participants that they do not identify with the group and resist its objective. After the "forming group" -stage all members of the groups, except one, adhered to the groups' objective of alleviating loneliness.

The objective should be clarified during the first session by discussing it (loneliness in our case). This can be aided, e.g. by applying activating methods such as art exercises. We used cards with images of pieces of art expressing various dimensions of loneliness (Blomqvist et al. 2007). This helped initiate discussions concerning loneliness. The facilitators' task is to discuss the common rules for group work, such as confidentiality and secrecy about other participants' personal matters, equal participation, and adherence to the groups' function (Toseland 1990). These were highlighted to our group facilitators. The basic task and secure structure — rules — can be seen as factors protecting the group (Harrison 1994, Pritchard & Pritchard 1999).

Group facilitators should understand that participants also experience hidden negative emotions during the "forming group" and "the honeymoon - finding "team spirit" -stages. Disclosing these feelings is desirable for fostering group development. The group facilitators can promote this by creating a secure environment, encouraging the expression of feelings and requesting feedback. In this sense, participants expressing critical and negative feelings are rather a strength than a challenge in promoting group development. The negative emotions and critics bring in "the real life", which participants can then experience in a safe way. Group facilitators should be able to act in a constructive way — as adults — in conflict situations and understand that criticism, and power game are normal in a group's developmental process. The group facilitator should step back at the "effectively working group" -stage, sufficiently hand over power and responsibility to group participants, so that the group could progress naturally to the "self-directed group" -stage. In many cases, the responsibility of the group facilitator is to remind participants at a sufficiently early stage about the end of the group meetings and prepare the group for the end, so that group members have time to mourn.

Other Special Features in Lonely Older People's Groups

Other special characteristics were detected in the lonely older people's groups. Some might be features occurring in all older people's groups (diseases, heterogenic functional status), and some are unique for these types of loneliness groups (commitment difficulties, reluctance to discuss loneliness), some are unique for art groups (the courage to try new things with the support of the group and surpass personal limits, being moved by art experiences, avoiding conversations about diseases), some are unique for exercise groups (eroticism, competition between group members), and some phenomena might be specific for several group types (flirting, a common secret of the group, a common enemy increasing group cohesion).

Typical characteristics of all our groups' were *diseases and heterogenic functional status,* which has also received attention in previous literature (Burnside & Schmidt 1994). This feature influenced the groups' functioning in several ways. Participants were heterogenic in their functional status despite special attention given to homogeneity when selecting the participants for the groups. Heterogeneity increases along with aging, and this was also observed in our groups. Functioning difficulties were not obstacles for participating in the art groups, but the group had to split up into subgroups when going on excursions, so that participants walking slowly could come along. In this sense, two professional facilitators in each group were essential.

The poor hearing of some participants additionally complicated their full participation in group conversations, and group facilitators had to make special arrangements to ensure the equality of members with hearing problems. Facilitators frequently sat next to participants with hearing problems and repeated important things of the conversations to them or presented direct questions to them. On the other hand, in this way they could control the group function in other respects as well.

> "We proposed that each one of us would listen to one speaker at a time, because all extra sounds could disturb those with hearing aids".

Each group had at least one member suffering from cognitive decline. This impaired their attention and ability to concentrate in the group work and discussions. When selecting participants for older people's groups it is desirable to find as homogeneous a group as possible in respect to physical and cognitive functioning as well as for the common objective of participating in the group (Toseland 1990). Groups have been arranged solely for participants with dementia (David 1991, Burnside & Schmidt 1994), but researchers have proposed that in favor of the groups' functioning, patients at different stages of dementia should not be included in the same groups (Toseland 1990, Evans et al. 2001). Participants in our groups were very discreet towards group members with memory problems and they received special attention. The groups worked well even if one participant had memory problems, but group functioning seemed to worsen if several demented members participated in the same group.

> "This was probably the third or fourth time that P. told the same stories. And the group still doesn't look down on her but listens quietly, just like the stories would be new."

Diseases influenced group functioning in other ways. Some participants in several groups did not show up to group meetings because of falling ill. Some participants were admitted to hospital and others went for rehabilitation. Some participants attended the sessions while either very tired or sick. They did not want to miss any of the meetings. Because of this, the group facilitators had to occasionally act as nurses.

> "I took W. to a public health nurse, because he had a fever. He had felt sick in the morning, but did not want to stay home."

Some participants suffered from fluctuations in alertness. Sometimes they were active during meetings and involved in group activities, but during some meetings they were tired and absent. Taking into consideration that diseases were present in all groups, it is surprising that they were discussed very rarely, according to analysis based on the diaries. In fact participants in some groups *avoided discussions concerning diseases.*

> ”Z. believes that a good attribute of this group is that you don’t have to listen to disease histories. According to him they are too commonly reported when older people of their age meet.”

Reluctance to discuss disease occurred in the art groups. One group named themselves the "stimulus group", in which diseases should be forgotten. This is an interesting phenomenon, as it has been argued that diseases are the most common conversation themes in older people's groups (Toseland 1990, Evans et al. 2001).

Participants appeared to enjoy *reminiscing and sharing mutual experiences.* A significant and special meaning of sharing and understanding experiences with someone of the same age was observed in all groups. The themes of reminiscing varied from one group to another. Some shared experiences from their childhood or sports achievements. More serious topics were also remembered in other groups, such as becoming widowed or being left alone. Reminiscing is said to be the most central conversation topic in older people's groups (Toseland 1990, Burnside & Schmidt 1994).

> ”Childhood-related homework was performed by a larger number of participants than ever before…pictures were only a part of the lively conversation.”

Loneliness was a discussion topic in all groups. During the group facilitator training sessions we discussed how elderly people might feel about sharing experiences concerning their loneliness in the group. The group facilitators felt uncomfortable bringing up the topic. We therefore created a tool for discussing the various aspects of loneliness using art cards (Blomqvist et al. 2007). Loneliness was a major discussion topic in most groups already during the first session. With loneliness cards the older people were able to lively discuss the different aspects of loneliness.

> ”It was surprising to deal with loneliness by using art images. Many group members openly discussed the difficult incidents that had occurred during their lives.”

Discussing loneliness was not easy for everyone. Dealing with the topic through art was easier for some participants. Some denied suffering from loneliness and others wanted to joke about the topic.

> "G. mentioned that he is not lonely. H. said that they are taught to be old in this group."

Discussing loneliness became easier with time in each group. Participants were even able to joke about themselves concerning this topic and they even competed with others in drawing attention to themselves by using this topic.

> "R. and S. "quarreled" about which one was more lonely. R. mentioned that S. has someone, but she herself doesn't have anyone. S. replied: I don't have anyone, now I have this group, which I have waited for the entire week."

Loneliness experiences were discussed from numerous viewpoints, as participants' experiences were very different. Several were widowed. Losing a spouse or another close person, even a child was discussed thoroughly. On the other hand, it was apparent to everyone that different people can experience loneliness in very different ways. In this respect participants tolerated the others' views well, accepted each other, and were discrete towards each other.

The participants' varying ways of approaching and experiencing loneliness created special challenges for the group facilitators in many ways. They had to be comfortable in elaborating and asking delicate questions about loneliness when participants brought up the topic. They had to be sensitive and give participants space when needed while giving the impression that participants are understood and accepted. Group facilitators additionally had to be sensitive if participants had difficulties with their feelings or there was resistance in the group. In other words they had to be sensitive in understanding when talking and asking additional questions was appropriate and when dismissing the topic was more diplomatic.

All in all, participants were very committed to their groups and the common objectives of alleviating loneliness and building friendships. A group's ability to attract members is said to dependent on how well it is able to satisfy the needs of its participants (Lenneer-Axelson & Thylefors 1998) and how clearly the group objective has been presented to the participants (Perraud et al. 2004). In this sense the leaders were very successful. The groups felt that they had a common task — alleviating loneliness. We knew before the intervention began that people suffering from loneliness might experience difficulties in adherence. These people may have experienced abandonment or feelings of being an outsider, and might therefore have difficulties trusting other people. In one Swedish study with similar older people's groups, 40% of the participants dropped out of the intervention (Andersson 1984, 1985). In fact, our group facilitators wrote about these issues in their diaries. Some participants showed *difficulties in adhering to their group.* Some participants had a need to be separated from others, others seemed to experience feelings of being an outsider, and each group had participants with difficulties engaging themselves with the group.

> ”I was somewhat nervous about U.’s response after the first session. She seemed to be suspicious and maybe a little ’sulky’”.

Some participants obviously attended the first meeting only to see what the group activity was about.

> ”K. was the one, who at the first meeting was the first to tell that he will no attend next time and that he is not lonely.”

Several participants were absent from the group sessions and in this way showed their difficulty engaging with the group. Absences were more common at the beginning of the intervention. Participants' weak adherence appeared to impact the entire group process. Other group members in some groups waited for and asked after the absent person, and the group felt incomplete without the missing person. Others felt insulted if one participant discontinued the group (this happened in two groups). They felt they were not good enough for the one who left the group. Participants pressured members planning to leave so that they would continue.

> ”D. said that she would not attend the excursion, as she had visited the place before. Others muttered and remarked that escaping in such a manner wasn’t allowed, and that replacement was not an option as they had already gotten used to D.”

We interpreted that a group’s social control can sometimes be too strong, and can act against itself. It can even lead to the dropping out of a group member. According to Toseland (1990), a group member may resolve experiences of losing their freedom derived from the social control of the group by leaving the group. However, single cases have shown how important it is that group facilitators pay attention to participant adherence, and support it in a delicate manner. This requires special professional skills from the group facilitators. However, the situations can sometimes be beyond their intervention. Adherence and absences have been recognized as threats for group cohesion (Perraud et al. 2004).

Art group participants in particular supported each other in *overcoming their limits and trying new things.* Several participants probably performed various tasks under the art theme for the first time in their lives, e.g. writing poetry, acting, and painting. This courage to try new things is partly related to a permissive and supportive attitude in the group, but art as a tool also seems to affect people, shake their attitudes, and get participants to open up themselves and jointly reflect on their experiences. Art touched the participants and they were affected by art experiences and had the courage to show it as well by sharing experiences with each other. This might have had an impact when participants ventured to overcome their own limits and the feeling of connectedness developed in the group.

The group can have a *mutual secret,* which may be related to tension between participants or to their earlier relationships. The secret can be shared between two or three members and later on between several group participants. Mutual agreement exists that the secret cannot be talked about. An uncovered and denied topic of conversation can hinder the activity and development of the group. This phenomenon was observed in one group, which was formed in a small community. We randomized the participants, so as not to effect who would be participating in the groups. One group had two siblings who did not get along with each other. They did not want to reveal that they are relatives, but instead pretended that they did not know each other. This affected the development of the entire group (group 3 in Table 2).

We observed an interesting phenomenon in two groups, which was that the groups had a *mutually experienced disappointment* with the group program. According to the group participants the program underestimated them. This disappointment was discussed, the group facilitators were criticized, and the producer of the disappointment received a 'common enemy' -label by the group. It appears that dealing with a mutual disappointment can make the group more connected and uniform. An 'unsuccessful' art program can in this way work as a rallying point for the group.

Flirting between women and men and joking had special meaning in the groups. This was detected in five art groups, although clear romances between participants did not develop during the group process. In the art groups, flirting might have been related to *the basic assumption group* described by Bion (Bion 2000, Lenneer-Axelson & Thylefors 1998). According to Bion, one out of three basic assumption groups is the "couple making group", in which two members of the group form a couple. The atmosphere of this group is hopeful, waiting, and also erotic in some sense. Hope for the future is essential to this kind of group. Sometimes the main aim of the group can be forgotten in a "couple making" group (Bion 2000, Lenneer-Axelson & Thylefors 1998). Our art groups can be recognized as future oriented, as the hope of friendship development was a central characteristic in each art group and the role of the official facilitator diminished towards the end of the groups' life courses.

Participants in several groups paid more attention to how they looked, and dressed up more for the group meetings towards the end of the sessions. Group facilitators commented in their diaries about the change in clothing and how participants visited hairdressers. Participants found it important that they were noticed, and their dressing up was also a message of respect to other members. This phenomenon has previously been observed in older people's groups (Burnside & Schmidt 1994).

This erotic feeling was even more prominent in the exercise groups. The erotic atmosphere was visible in several ways. Bawdy jokes were a typical characteristic of inside humor experienced in each exercise group. Positive tension existed between the female and male participants. Joyful flirting occurred between participants in four groups. A nascent romance was observed in two groups, and other participants supported it. Surprisingly open physical touching occurred in a couple of groups. The group facilitators were confused about this and did not know how to confine it without hurting anyone's feelings.

> "U. and O. were openly a couple today…they even considered engagement.. They had the most impossible play going on concerning their future plans. They enjoyed the attention given to them and that they were able to amuse the others…"
> ".. picked Y. up the floor [to dance], and it could be seen how Y. shone because of the attention. When she came back, Y. whooped to us, asking if we got jealous!"

Each exercise group had both men and women participants. Dancing, physical touch, and listening to one's own bodily emotions with the aid of physical exercise obviously brought up erotic needs and hopes in participants. The flirting and bawdy humor pleasantly supported our aim of the intervention: the building of relationships and alleviating loneliness. However, might one's happiness be another's grief? Do the other group members feel even more lonely when seeing others finding pairs? This is possible, but the diaries do not give a direct answer to this. Maybe these romances drew so much of our facilitators' attention that the letdowns of the other participants were ignored?

Competitive elements related to sports were evident in the exercise groups. Exercises and plays to some extent provoked *competition between the participants.* Mild but seriously-taken competition existed between group members in two groups. Losing a competition in front of the group can be experienced as losing face, even if it is just a playful game. A competitive attitude can be a threat for group cohesion and its mutual task. Earlier exercise studies have shown that competition and a class-like atmosphere may hinder some people from participating in exercise groups (King 2001). Competition is culturally and naturally related to exercise, which is challenging for group facilitators. Sports performance has been measured since elementary school, and schoolchildren's achievements have been compared with the respective performance of others. This may have created traumas in self-respect and repulsive attitudes towards exercise among many of us. Group facilitators should take this into account so that all participants can feel recognized and competent as themselves (Sorensen et al. 1999, Ojanen et al. 2001). Focusing on achievements in sports can be a burden, as some participants may feel even more like outsiders (Ojanen et al. 2001, Salmon 2001). Exercise additionally exposes the limits of our bodies to ourselves and others, which may sometimes diminish motivation (Salmon 2001).

> "P. made a sharp comment at the beginning of the group discussion, that if fatness is a conversation topic for today, she would go home straight away."

In this respect it is understandable that *discrimination* may also occur in older people's groups. In such situations facilitators should take an active and controlling role. They should offer support so that object of discrimination is not left outside the group or discriminated by some dominant participants.

GROUP ROLES

Participants assumed roles in respect to the group. Some participants had one clear role, whereas others had several roles during the course of the group process. The position of "***leader***" was taken by one group member in 10 of the groups. She/he was the one who took responsibility when something had to be organized. The participants of one group offered the leader's role to one group member, who refused to take it.

"L. turned out to be the leading spirit of the group. She concentrated on the task, was enthusiastic, analyzed it, and inspired others to join in."

One person in each group took the role of ***"critic",*** and acted as the antennae of group vibrations. She/he was the one who dared to criticize the program or tell the facilitators about worries on her/his mind.

"When J. criticized last session's program with harsh words the others looked subtly at me how I would react."

The conflict stage of the groups was interesting. Besides receiving criticism, the facilitators also experienced some rebellions. Participants refused to perform common tasks or participate properly.

Each group had members who would create the *"team spirit"*. Some groups even had two or three such persons. These individuals openly stated that they appreciated the group, and verbalized common positive feelings experienced by the group. They gave significance to the group's feelings.

"S. put her arm on M.'s shoulder and said that we are similar in spirit."

Each group had one or two members who were *silent.* Most of them were very attentive and good listeners, and began opening up when the security of the group increased.

"V. said that before her disease she used to be talkative, but that she had become a little scared of talking because she had problems finding words."

A total of ten groups had one person each, who *underlined his/her dissimilarity.* This individual brought up the differences in his/her life situation compared to others. These persons were bystanders at the beginning of the group's life course, but became well attached as the group process progressed.

"He said that he is so autonomous that he wants to eat alone. He said he is used to eating alone."

Facilitators should be able to tailor group programs so that they interest and challenge everyone. Ignoring the silent ones and the bystanders would be easy. Facilitators should be aware that such persons exist in older people's groups and techniques have been developed for participating them (Burnside and Schmidt 1994).Very *talkative and dominant* individuals are also challenging group members, who take a lot of space from others. Their feelings may regulate the entire atmosphere of the group. The facilitators were instructed to use special techniques in controlling these persons.

> "F. began telling a story. P. did not have the patience to listen, but instead began simultaneously telling her own stories. Fortunately I was sitting beside her, and could interrupt her and urge her to listen."

There were also *humorous persons* in four groups. They told jokes and made the group laugh a lot. Some also *accompanied* them, the leaders or dominating persons. They chimed in to the others actions and supported them.

Some groups had a *disabled or sick* person who created a need in others to take care of him/her. It appears that this person took the sick role so that the entire group could project their feelings and fears.

It was important for the atmosphere that groups consisted of both men and women. The males — being a minority — often had a central role in most groups and the females supported this. We wished to avoid groups with only one man, because we did not want a situation with one "king" among many women. However, a second man refused to attend one group and, therefore, that group only had one man. The men's dominant role in older people's groups has been noticed in previous studies (de Medeiros et al. 2007). Their study suggested that men might bring a competitive atmosphere to the groups. Our study suggests that they also stimulate interaction and flirting between members.

Group processess and being a group member provokes various roles in relation to the group and the other members (Lenneer-Axelsson & Thylefors 1998). This also occurs in older people's groups. Previous studies have distinguished the typical roles of "dominant", "controller" or "messenger" (Toseland 1990, Lenneer-Axelsson & Thylefors 1998). Group roles may emphasize or caricature a person's special features.

On the other hand, groups need these roles. A group may choose the leader, bystander or critic from its members. Group therapy uses the concept of projective identification in this respect (Kajamaa 1996). In projective identification the group members identify some uncomfortable feature of themselves, and place it on others. The receiver of the role may be guided or even pressed to act according to that role. This phenomenon may also take place when the group has a scapegoat or when the group focuses on caring for one of its members as if that member is the only one suffering from disabilities.

Facilitators should be aware of these phenomena. A skilled facilitator can take advantage of them or she/he can experience them as challenges. For example, facilitators may experience the *'leader'* of the group as a competitor, whereas at best this *'leader'* can promote the group process towards self-direction. The *'critic'* in the group may be experienced as a threat or creator of discord, whereas in fact that person is usually the one who helps encourage the group to solve its problems. The critic helps the group tolerate conflicts, which is essential for the creative process of the group (Lenneer-Axelsson & Thylefors 1998).

What Promotes the Developmental Process Towards an Effectively Working and Self-Directed Group?

Mutual friendship building and alleviation of loneliness were the group objectives. Four out of six art groups and one out of six exercise groups continued the group meetings independently after the official sessions were over. Maturation of each group continued until the end. More than two out of three participants (69%) felt they had gained new friends after the group meetings. What made this happen?

According to Lenneer-Axelson and Thylefors (1998), specific characteristics exist in well-operating "ideal groups", which create an especially allowing atmosphere and permit the group to efficiently work for a common objective. These characteristics include the groups' good self-esteem or identity, clear and different views allowing for interaction, humor, acceptance of differences, tolerance of conflicts, and each group members' responsibility of taking part in the group tasks. All our groups were permissive and liberal. There was tolerance for conflicts, humor, and happiness as well. All took responsibility for the groups' basic tasks of alleviating loneliness and promoting friendships. Four groups clearly had their own identity. A mutual secret probably hindered communication in one group. Furthermore, competitiveness diminished the equality and mutual support in some exercise groups.

It can be assumed that a particularly well-functioning and self-directed group activates its members socially, and in this sense promoting the independence of the group is an essential objective for group activity in lonely older people's groups. We therefore trained our professionals in the groups to act more as facilitators than as leaders. We wished the social actions and communication to happen between the older people and not between professionals and participants. However, the development to a self-directed group seemed to only partly be attributable to the group facilitator's actions, while also partly depending on situation-specific matters, e.g. suitable persons being selected to the same group. Group facilitators must be professionals, and familiar and confident with group developmental stages and the different roles group members can take. Promoting the development of the group requires quite small and smooth interventions from the group facilitators. Participants' feelings of safety and equality should be promoted. This requires that the sessions have a clear structure and that common rules and the mutual task are verbalized. Participants will not adhere to the group without a mutual task and objective (to alleviate loneliness) (Toseland 1990). Above all, facilitators should be able to withdraw themselves to the background and give opportunity, encouragement, and responsibility to the group, when it is ready for it.

To mature to the stage of a self-directed group, a group needs a person from its members who takes responsibility and leadership in organizing future plans and meetings. This kind of *'leader'* was found in five groups. Group spirit and attachment are greatly dependent on *the "team spirit"* creators inside the group, who verbalize the positive emotions of the group. The impact of this type of member has been identified as a promoter of group cohesion (Perraud et al. 2004). A group additionally also needs an honest ***'critic'*** from within its ranks. A critical member gives the possibility for diversity — allowing both 'good' and 'bad' participants to concurrently exist in the group. She/he also creates an atmosphere-within the group where participants are "living a real life" within the group, and are not just polite but distant people, who happen to participate in same activities. A critic creates space and tolerance for conflicts, which are preconditions for group creativity (Lenneer-Axelson & Thylefors 1998).

It appears that coincidences may hinder group functioning. These kinds of factors could be the heterogeneity of a group, difficulties in adhering to objectives because of a group member's own life situation or painful events earlier in life. Adherence to the groups' mutual objective appears to be essential to all participants. The poor adherence of even only one member will influence the functioning and self-esteem of the entire group. Special attention should be given to selection and potential commitment when recruiting and gathering group members.

RELIABILITY OF THE STUDY FINDINGS

The reliability and validity of the study design, data and their analyses were confirmed in several ways (Silverman 2000). The main data source consisted of the group facilitators' diaries. Half of the diaries were descriptions of group activities, which included objectives for each group meeting and evaluations of how this objective was achieved. The other half was reflections of the facilitators' impressions on group moods, relationships between participants, and also the group facilitator's own actions. For half of the group meetings we received the diaries of both group facilitators of each group. In addition, we had a possibility to visit and observe 2/12 group sessions in each group. We therefore had several different views on the groups. These gave us quite a good picture of what happened in the groups. The two facilitators might have remembered things that the other had not written about. Acquiring two sets of diaries was our goal, so as to be able to examine phenomenon of the group from different angles. We additionally visited the groups as observers and could confirm that the diaries were in line with what really happened according to our opinion. The same triangulation of the methods and data was used with data from the first postal questionnaire and the first study measurement of all participants.

Analysis reliability of the data was secured using three independent researchers. Reliability was secured after the first analysis phase by comparing the coding made by the researchers and discussing the differences.

How equivalent the descriptions in the diaries are in relation to reality can be questioned. Simple event descriptions tell very little about the feelings and moods of the groups. On the other hand, the reflective diaries are already the writers' interpretations of the events. The views of two people and descriptions from two different perspectives complete each other and enhance the validity of the data. We additionally had a total of 12 group facilitators, so we have several different kinds of descriptions and interpretations of the groups. This also improves the validity of our data. However, it is possible that group facilitators do not always wish or remember to describe things, which they do not consider relevant or where their own role would be presented in an unfavorable light. We can quite reliably interpret from the data that events described are real phenomena occurring in the groups, but it is much more difficult to draw conclusions about "missing phenomenon". Were discussions on disease really missing from the group conversations or did the leaders just not report on them? Were there only a few conflicts in the groups or were some not reported? Another problem in the data may be that the facilitators' might experience a conscious or unconscious need to please the researchers and transact data that they think to be equivalent to the researchers needs. The training given to facilitators concerning group dynamics may in this sense have influenced the interpretations and selections of what was written in their diaries. Using this data we can approach the reality of the groups, but we cannot gain an exact picture.

Conclusion

The group dynamics and phenomena emerging in the group facilitators' diaries and in our observations were quite surprising in their familiarity. Similar phenomena have also been detected in other adult groups. These findings shake our attitudes towards aging. The older people's personal characteristics and humanity are visible in the findings. The basic needs for human relationships and other people's acceptance and caring are the same and universally human despite high age.

References

Agronin M. Group therapy in older adults. Curr Psychiatry Rep 2009;11:27-32.

Andersson L. Intervention against loneliness in a group of elderly women: a process evaluation. *Human Relations* 1984;37:295-310.

Andersson L. Intervention against loneliness in a group of elderly women – an impact evaluation. *Soc Sci Med* 1985;58:683-95.

Barlow J, Wright C, Sheasby J, Turner A, Hainsworth J. Self-management approaches for people with chronic conditions: a review. Patient Educ Couns 2002;48:177-87.

Bodenheimer T, Lorig K, Holman H, Grunbach K: Patient self-management of chronic disease in primary care. *JAMA* 2002;288:2469-75.

Bion WR. *Experiences in groups and other papers.* Rouledge. London and New York, 2000.

Blomqvist L, Pitkälä K, Routasalo P. Images of loneliness: using art as an educational method in professional training. *J Contin Educ Nurs* 2007;38:89-93.

Bowers BJ, Fibich B, Jacobson N. Care-as-service, care-as-relating, care-as-comfort: understanding nursing home residents' definitions of quality. *Gerontologist* 2001;41:539-45.

Burnside I, Schmidt MG. Working with older adults. *Group Process and techniques.* Third Edition. Jones and Bartlett Publishers. Sudbury, Massachusetts, 1994.

Christensen U, Schmidt L, Budtz-Jørgensen E, Avlund K. Group cohesion and social support in exercise classes: results from a danish intervention study. *Health Educ Behav* 2006;33:677-89.

Clark WG, Vorst VR. Group therapy with chronically depressed geriatric patients. *J Psychosoc Nurs Ment Health Serv* 1994;32:9-13.

Cockman P, Evans B, Raynolds P. *Client-centred consulting.* McGraw-Hill Book Company. Lontoo, 1992.

David P. Effectiveness of group work with the cognitively impaired older adult. *Am J Alzheimer Care Related Disord Res* 1991;6:10-6.

Ettin MF, Cohen BD, Fidler JW. *Group-as-a-whole theory viewed in its 20th-century context. Group dynamics: Theory, Research, and Practice* 1997;1:329-40.

Evans S, Chisholm P, Walshe J. A dynamic psychotherapy group for the elderly. *Group Analysis* 2001;34:287-98.

Folstein MF, Folstein SE, McHugh PR. "Mini-mental state". A practical method for grading the cognitive state of patients for the clinician. *J Psychiatr Res* 1975;12:189-98.

Gorey KM, Cryns AG. Group work as interventive modality with the older depressed client: a meta-analytic view. *J Gerontol Soc Work* 1991;16:137-57.

Harrison MI. A guide to diagnosing behavior during meetings. Teoksessa: Harrison MI. *Diagnosing organizations. Methods, models and processes. Sage Publications.* Thousand Oaks, London, New Delhi,1994.

Husaini BA, Cummings S, Kilbourne B, Roback H, Sherkat D, Levine R, Cain VA. Group therapy for depressed elderly women. *Int J Group Psychother* 2004;54:295-319.

Kajamaa R. Projective identification in human relationships and in psychotherapy. In: Arppo M, Pölönen R, Sitolahti T. *Basics in group psychotherapy.* (In Finnish) Yliopistopaino. Helsinki, 1996, pp. 47-57.

King AC. Interventions to promote physical activity by older adults. *J Gerontol A Biol Sci Med Sci 2001*;56:S36-46.

Laakkonen ML, Pitkala KH, Strandberg TE. Terminally ill elderly person's experiences, attitudes and needs – a qualitative study. *OMEGA* 2004;49:117-29.

Lavoie JP. Support groups for informal caregivers don't work. Refocus the groups or the evaluations? *Can J Aging* 1995;14:580-603.

Lenneer-Axelson B, Thylefors I. The psychology of the work group. A book about teamwork. *Joint Industrial Safety Council.* Ljungby, 1998.

Luft J. Group processes. An introduction to group dynamics. *Mayfield Publishing Company.* Palo Alto, CA, 1970.

Marriott A, Donaldson C, Tarrier N, Burns A. Effectiveness of cognitive-behavioural family intervention in reducing the burden of care in carers of patients with Alzheimer's disease. *Br J Psychiatry* 2000;176:557-62.

Martin PY, Turner BA. Grounded theory and organizational research. *J Appl Behav Sci* 1986;22:141-57.

de Medeiros K, Harris-Trovato D, Bradley E, Gaines J, Parrish J. Group dynamics in a discussion group for older adults: does gender play a role? *Educ Gerontol* 2007;33:111-25.

Ojanen M, Svennvig H, Nyman M, Halme J. Exercise in a right way - and feel well. Significance of exercise for well-being. Liikuntatieteellisen Seuran julkaisu nro 153. Helsinki, 2001 (in Finnish).

Payne KT, Marcus DK. The efficacy of group therapy for older adult clients: a meta-analysis. *Group Dynamics: Theory Res Pract* 2008;12:268-78.

Perraud S, Farran CJ, Loukissa D, Paun O. Alzheimer's disease caregiving information and skills, part III: group process issues and concerns. *Res Nurs Health* 2004;27:110-20.

Pitkala KH, Blomqvist L, Routasalo R, Karvinen E, Oikarinen U, Saarenheimo M, Mantyranta T. Leading groups of older people: Description and evaluation of education of professionals. *Educ Gerontol* 2004;30:821-34.

Pitkala KH, Routasalo P, Kautiainen H, Tilvis RS. Effects of psychosocial group rehabilitation on health, use of health care services, and mortality of older persons suffering from loneliness: a randomized, controlled trial. *J Gerontol* 2009;64:792-800.

Pitkala KH, Routasalo P, Kautiainen H, Tilvis RS. Effects of socially stimulating group intervention on lonely older people's cogntion – a randomized controlled trial. *Am J Geriatr Psychiatr* 2011;19:654-663.

Pritchard P, Pritchard J. *Tiimistä toimeen terveydenhuollossa.* Edita, Helsingin kansanterveystieteen laitos. Helsinki, 1999.

Routasalo P, Pitkala K. Loneliness among older people. Rev Clin Gerontol 2003;13:303-11.

Routasalo PE, Savikko N, Tilvis RS, Strandberg TE, Pitkälä KH. Social contacts and their relationship to loneliness among aged people - a population-based study. *Gerontology* 2006;52:181-7.

Routasalo P, Tilvis RS, Kautiainen H, Pitkala KH. Effects of psychosocial group rehabilitation on social functioning, loneliness and psychological well-being of lonely older people. A randomized, controlled trial. *J Adv Nurs* 2009;65:297-305.

Saiger GM. Group psychotherapy with older adults. *Psychiatry* 2001;64:132-45.

Salmon P. Effects of physical exercise on anxiety, depression, and sensitivity to stress: a unifying theory. *Clin Psychol Rev* 2001;21:33-61.

Savikko N; Routasalo P, Tilvis S, Pitkälä K. Psychosocial group rehabilitation for lonely older people: a description of intervention and participants' feedback. *Int J Older People's Nurs* 2010;5:16-24.

Shulman SC. Psychodynamic group therapy with older women. *Social Casework* 1985; 66: 579-86.

Schmidt GL, Keyes B. Group psychotherapy with family caregivers of demented patients. *Gerontologist* 1985;25:347-50.

Silverman D. *Doing Qualitative Research: A Practical Handbook.* Sage Publications, London, 2000.

Sorensen M, Anderssen S, Hjerman I, Holme I, Ursin H. The effect of exercise and diet on mental health and quality of life in middle-aged individuals with elevated risk factors for cardiovascular disease. *J Sports Sci* 1999;17:369-77.

Stewart M, Craig D, MacPherson K, Alexander S. Promoting positive affect and diminishing loneliness of widowed seniors through a support intervention. *Public Health Nurs* 2001;18:54-63.

Tilvis RS, Pitkala KH, Jolkkonen J, Strandberg TE. Social networks and dementia. *Lancet* 2000;356:77-8.

Tilvis RS, Laitala V, Routasalo PE, Pitkälä KH. Suffering from loneliness indicates significant mortality risk of older people. *J Aging Res* 2011;2011:534781. doi: 10.4061/2011/534781.

Toseland RW, Rossiter CM, Labrecque MS. The effectiveness of peer-led and professionally led groups to support family caregivers. *Gerontologist* 1989;29:465-71.

Toseland RW. *Group work with older adults.* New York University Press. New York and London, 1990.

Toseland RW, Rivas RF. Understanding group dynamics. Chapter 3. In: Toseland RW, Rivas RF. *An introduction to group work practice.* Allyn & Bacon. Boston 2005. pp. 64-91.

Tuckman BW. Developmental sequence in small groups. *Psychol Bull* 1965;63:384-99.

Weiner MB, Weinstock CS. Group progress of community elderly as measured by tape recordings, group tempo and group evaluation. *Int J Aging Human Develop* 1979-80;10:177-85.

In: Group Therapy
Editor: Hellen Derrickson

ISBN: 978-1-63463-173-0

Chapter 4

GROUP TREATMENT FOR CHRONIC LOW BACK PAIN: THEORY, PRACTICE AND EFFECTIVENESS

Carla Vanti**, MSc, PT, OMT, Silvia Borghi, PT, OMT, and Paolo Pillastrini, MSc, PT

[1]Adjunct Professor Manual Therapy,
Department of Biomedical and Neuromotor Sciences,
Alma Mater Studiorum University of Bologna, Bologna, Italy
[2]Clinical Tutor Masters in Manual Therapy and Musculoskeletal Rehabilitation, Department of Biomedical Sciences,
University of Padova, Padova, Italy
[3]Associate Professor Department of Biomedical and Neuromotor Sciences,
Alma Mater Studiorum University of Bologna, Bologna, Italy

ABSTRACT

Background: Rehabilitation in musculoskeletal disorders through group treatment is commonly cited in literature, especially so in the last ten years, despite the fact that the contents and the characteristics of these programs are poorly documented.

---

* Via Tosarelli 144 40055 Castenaso (Bologna) Italy, Phone: +39051785254 Fax +39051785254 Mobile +39335475464, e-mail address: carla.vanti@unibo.it.

The aims of this chapter are: 1) to perform a narrative review on the cognitive behavioral approach and on group treatments for chronic low back pain (LBP), 2) to propose a "multimodal group program" model and to explain its application in different chronic spinal dysfunctions and diseases (disc degeneration, arthritis, spinal stenosis, anatomical and clinical instability), and 3) to show an example of this type of group treatment.

Methods: A narrative review of literature was performed on the basis of current evidence. The "multimodal group program" proposal was based on recent knowledge about the mechanical, neurophysiological and behavioral components of chronic spinal pain.

Finally, methods for the practical example were the following:

Sample: six subjects with chronic LBP (lasting at least three months)

Treatment: 10 weekly one-hour sessions

Outcome measures: Numerical Rating Scale (NRS), Oswestry Disability Index – Italian Version (ODI –I), Roland & Morris Disability Questionnaire (RMDQ), Tampa Scale for Kinesiophobia (TSK), and Short-Form Health Survey Questionnaire (SF-36)

Timing: outcome measures were administered at baseline and at the end of the ten sessions.

Discussion: The group treatment we propose is defined as "multimodal" because during each meeting, a physical therapist incorporates some specific exercises with information and practical training on correct postures and movements. Moreover, explanation about the mechanisms for onset and persistence of pain and about the different strategies to manage it (through exercise, relaxation and active coping strategies) is a fundamental part of the program.

This group treatment includes different physical therapy strategies (joint mobilization, muscle strengthening, coordination and balance exercises, stretching, and so on) and a psychological approach, to modify beliefs and behaviors and to reduce the need for individual treatment.

PART ONE - INTRODUCTION

Low back pain (LBP) is a very common clinical condition, affecting both genders and most age groups [1]. It is related to relevant social and economic costs for individuals, work environments and society [2]. The one-year prevalence of a first episode of LBP is calculated as being from 6.3% to 15.4%, while the one-year prevalence of a subsequent episode of LBP ranges from 1.5% to 36% [3]. The percentage of remission at one year ranges from 54% to 90%, while recurrences at one year range from 24% to 80% [4].

LBP is classified as acute, sub-acute or chronic, depending on the duration of pain. Commonly LBP is categorized as acute (or brief) when it lasts up to four weeks, sub-acute (or longer) from four to twelve weeks and chronic (long-lasting) when it lasts more than twelve weeks [5].

Only 33% of patients recovers within the first 3 months, and 65% of patients has pain at one year. If the complete absence of pain is adopted as a criterion, this percentage rises to 71%, compared to 57% if broader criteria are used. As a consequence, according to Itz et al., [6], "*the assumption that spontaneous recovery occurs in a large majority of patients is not justified*". Previous episodes of LBP seem to be predictive for the onset of recurrence within a period of 12 months [7].

LBP is physiological (a vital symptom, a defense system) when it represents a tissue injury signal, which is essential to avoid damage. It becomes pathological when it is self-maintaining, losing the original meaning and becoming a peculiar condition of the individual [8].

It has been observed that brain structures undergo continuous reorganization in relation to the stimuli they receive [9]. In chronic LBP, central sensitization may occur and can provoke phenomena like hyperalgesia and allodynia. Synaptic activation in the somatosensory pathways increases and, at the same time, inhibition is reduced. This central amplification intensifies pain response to the nociceptive stimulus in terms of amplitude, duration, and spatial extension (hyperalgesia = increased pain response to a normally painful stimulus). Moreover, we can observe increased activation of some normally silent synapses that recruit subliminal inputs, such as low-threshold ones (allodynia = pain response to a stimulus that normally is not painful, for example lightly touching or rubbing) [10].

In chronic LBP, morphological and metabolic changes have been shown on the cerebral gray matter (e.g. atrophy), in relation to duration and intensity of pain. Due to the dynamic plasticity of the brain, these modifications are reversible through pain relief and specific rehabilitation [9].

Clinical criteria proposed by Smart et al. (2012) [11] to identify central sensitization are:

1. Pain out of proportion to the injury,
2. Aggravations without any apparent reason,
3. Presence of maladaptive psychosocial conditions,
4. Pain or tenderness in widespread and/or non-anatomical areas.

If all four clinical criteria are present, the probability for central sensitization to occur is equal to 40.6%.

Psychological and social factors act as pain reinforcement: in fact, a nociception that cannot be resolved does not alone explain the amplification of symptoms. Personal experience of pain is determined by affective and cognitive aspects, past experience, psychic structure, and socio-cultural factors [8].

Psychosocial factors are considered to be the strongest prognostic factors for LBP and contributing factors for slower or less complete recovery and persistent pain. These so-called yellow flags increase pain and disability and reduce the self-efficacy perception. Catastrophization, kinesiophobia, fear avoidance beliefs, passive coping and disuse syndrome appear as risk factors for the transition from acute to chronic LBP [12].

Catastrophic thinking is described as an exaggerated and negative mental condition associated with actual or anticipated pain experience. The consequences related to pain are amplified, with thoughts like "I will never heal", "I cannot go back to the way I was before", "I will not return to work", etc. [13]. Catastrophizing predicted the levels of pain and disability and mediated treatment efficacy in most studies; as a consequence, the presence of this condition should be considered in patients with persistent back pain [12].

Kinesiophobia refers to an irrational fear of physical movements resulting from feeling vulnerable to painful injury or new injury [14]. Fear of movement leads to the cultivation of negative thoughts, such as: "If I do physical activity, it could hurt me", and favors the disuse syndrome. According to Wertly et al., [12], *"evidence suggests that fear avoidance beliefs are prognostic for poor outcome in subacute LBP, and thus early treatment, including interventions to reduce fear avoidance beliefs, may avoid delayed recovery and chronicity."*

Passive coping is the behavior assumed due to fear of movement: the subject reduces or avoids the task as soon as he/she feels pain. Passive coping is favored by some misguided thoughts like: "My pain is caused by my work", "I have a hereditary problem", "I get hurt more easily than other people," and so on. In this pathological vicious cycle, each failure emphasizes the misguided thoughts, decrease in activity, and passive coping. Each failure also encourages behavior like staying at home, not resuming normal work, avoiding social contacts, and finally promotes anxiety and depression.

The main Guidelines stress the relevance of helping LBP subjects in managing their condition not only through specific exercises, but also with cognitive-behavioral changes [15]. Group Therapy and Cognitive-Behavioral approach are frequently used treatments for chronic/long-lasting LBP.

Part Two - Cognitive-Behavioral Approach to Chronic Pain. Concept, Strategies and Evidence of Efficacy

Musculoskeletal disorders may have more than one etiology, which are sometimes unknown. Nonspecific pain is frequently related to psychosocial factors, which also contribute to the development of symptoms towards chronic pain. According to the biopsychosocial model, one of the possible rehabilitation strategies is Cognitive Behavioral Therapy (CBT).

CBT is a branch of psychology including several therapeutic techniques born in the '60s in contrast to the psychodynamic model proposed by Sigmund Freud. CBT is based on the hypothesis that the mental perceptions and behavior of a subject are largely determined by the way in which he/she structures the world [16].

The main strategies and techniques of CBT are:

- Education and Information
- Relaxation techniques
- Problem solving strategies
- Pacing
- Graded exposure
  - *Graded exercise*
  - *Graded activity*
- Role playing
- Home-based exercise

Concerning education and information, first of all, the clinician helps patients to recognize their maladaptive behaviors and incorrect cognitions. An open discussion between clinician and subject can encourage the patient to elaborate different concepts and identify possible changes. In LBP patients, it is relevant to recognize which activities they avoid doing for fear of pain and gradually resume doing them [17].

Relaxation techniques like the so-called "Progressive Relaxation" and "Controlled Breathing" help obtain better control on some body functions, reduce muscular tension, improve the quality of sleep, and finally, control pain [18]. For example, to promote progressive relaxation, subject in supine position is asked to tense several areas of his/her body for five seconds and then to progressively decrease this tension. Subject is invited to feel the relaxing sensation for five seconds, and this sequence is repeated two/three times for each main muscular group [19]. Controlled breathing is used in combination with relaxation and aims to reduce breathing frequency and to augment the amplitude of diaphragm movements, with relaxed neck, shoulder and upper arms.

Problem-solving strategies aim to remove, circumvent or profitably use the obstacle that prevents achieving a goal. To obtain this objective, subject must first define the obstacle and the aim, then he/she should generate ideas and transform these ideas into practical solutions. Finally, subject must put these solutions into practice and verify their impact on daily living activities. These "problem-solving strategies" can be applied to each specific activity (e.g. housework, gardening, work, sports, etc.) [20].

Several authors proposed different problem-solving strategies. Pacing techniques aim to increase activity while avoiding the rest caused by excessive stress. Using these techniques, patients try to augment their activity levels each day, but within the limitations that their condition requires. Proper use of pacing techniques allows subject to stop an activity when he/she feels that he/she has reached a point beyond which pleasant fatigue becomes unpleasant. Subjects are led to better feel their body sensations and to recognize their limits. They are also encouraged to take a day off after having done hard and not preventable activities. Practical experience allows patients to understand the personal level of activity permitted without provoking symptoms and to manage different daily needs without exacerbating the clinical condition. For example, if the aim is to do housework, today he/she does one thing, tomorrow another and so on [20].

Graded exposure consists in programming behavior modification step by step. Patients are educated to reduce their fear of movement. At the same time, they receive positive reinforcement for performing activities they mistakenly believe are at risk and for improving active coping strategies. Obviously, it is not possible to separate the effects of education from those of activity implementation [21].

Graded exposure includes two different approaches: "*graded exercise*" and "*graded activity*".

Graded exercise is a sequence of different exercises, from lighter (unloading) to harder (loading) ones. Exercises are used as a cognitive tool to favor thought and behavior modification. They try to restore correct segmental and global movements, paying attention to movement quality and requesting repetitions, which allow subject to make a learned movement automatically and to increase endurance. This program is initially oriented to exercises, then to functional activities; progression concerns both the type of functional activity involved and the amount of imposed loads [22].

Graded activity seeks to find the maximum possible level of exercise/activity without provoking pain or tissue irritation. This baseline is below the discomfort threshold. After having established this level, subject and clinician can together build activity progression; when an activity becomes easy to do, it is increased (by about 20%). For example, if the aim is to take the subway to go back to work, this objective must be divided into small, easily reached steps and gradually achieved. The first day, subject goes to the subway platform without taking the train; the second day, he/she could take the train to the following stop, the third day, two stops, and so on. Patient is asked to do a hierarchy of activities he/she fears. Exposure starts with the less feared activity, and clinician helps patient to evaluate the exposure and its consequences. In this way, subject can face the non-rational and counter cognitions practically. When the negative associations have been eradicated, activities associated with higher anxiety levels are faced. At the end of the treatment, patient should maintain regular fitness activities to increase local and general loadibility [23].

Role playing is a method based on the simulation of a situation or an event. Due to the active involvement of the subject, it is considered an efficient, practical approach to modify cognition and behavior.

Home-based exercise is an opportunity to extend thought, emotion and behavior modifications obtained during physical therapy sessions beyond the therapeutic setting. Patient's adherence (active participation) to home treatments and ergonomic advice is considered a crucial point in maximizing the effectiveness of conservative treatments. Clinician's style and the content of exercise programs (time consumption, complexity and effects) seem to be relevant factors in improving patient adherence to home-based exercise [24].

Cognitive-behavioral strategies can be efficiently applied to physical therapy treatments for patients complaining of chronic pain. In this case, physical therapist uses strategies to reduce excessive patient attention on body sensations, to identify misguided and irrational beliefs and to make the patient aware of the ineffectiveness of passive strategies. Furthermore, physical therapist tries to modify patient behavior via effective "taking charge" and establishing shared goals.

Physical therapy oriented to cognitive-behavioral strategies is based on sharing time and methods between clinician and subject, and aims to reduce patient's dependency on passive and drug therapies. Some studies demonstrated that in physical therapy settings, in addition to information and education, some forms of support that can continue even after discharge must be provided. For example, periodic check-up meetings and the possibility to contact clinician when needed are commonly suggested [25].

Evidence of Efficacy

For patients with CLBP, a systematic review showed moderate quality evidence that in the short-term, operant therapy is more effective than waiting list and behavioral therapy is more effective than usual care for pain relief. However, no specific type of behavioral therapy appeared to be more effective than others [26]. This result was confirmed by Van Middelkoop et al. [27], who concluded that behavioral treatment was found to be effective in reducing pain intensity at short-term follow-up compared to no treatment/waiting list controls.

Positive results were found for gradually increased physical activity as compared to minimal intervention (general practitioner's care or exercises) for lumbar pain and disability. Some evidence showed that physical therapists generally lack the skills necessary to effectively implement an intervention on a psychological basis. A plan to manage the recurrences helps patients cope with the anxiety and fear of further injuries [28].

A randomized controlled trial showed that graded exercise and graded activity resulted equivalent in improving pain and disability in chronic LBP [29]. Moreover, surgery can be more effective than non-structured conservative treatments in chronic LBP; nevertheless, it is not more effective than structured cognitive-behavioral treatments [30].

A systematic review by Santandrea et al. [31] showed that positive results were found with respect to CBT effectiveness for nonspecific LBP and non-specific spinal pain. On the other hand, conflicting results were reported with regard to specific LBP. CBT was shown to have a better cost-effectiveness ratio, regardless of the spinal district in question. Considering economic advantage of CBT and the poor quality of available clinical trials, it is reasonable to argue that further clinical trials are necessary in order to study more uniform and reproducible CBT techniques. To conclude this paragraph, according to Frank et al. [32], we suggest that *"clinicians should know the availability of psychological treatments for pain in their practice setting, especially CBT, and refer patients earlier to providers or clinics that deliver CBT for low back pain"*.

PART THREE - GROUP TREATMENTS FOR CHRONIC LOW BACK PAIN. CONCEPT, STRATEGIES AND EVIDENCE OF EFFICACY

Group treatments for chronic LBP commonly include exercise, back schools, and patient education. These different therapeutic tools may be combined in multimodal treatments.

The effectiveness of Multimodal Group Programs (MGP) on subjects suffering from LBP is disputed. Despite the fact that some studies showed positive results in terms of frequency and intensity of LBP for interventions including training, education and exercise, other work obtained different results [33].

In primary care setting, small improvements in pain intensity [34] and moderate reduction of disability [35] were observed at one year follow-up. Nevertheless, more favorable results were found in private outpatient settings after community-based group exercise programs [36].

Exercise therapy is defined as "*a series of specific movements with the aim of training or developing the body by a routine practice or physical training to promote good physical health* [37]". Current literature provides some evidence for the effectiveness of different approaches as an extension-oriented treatment approach [38-40] or exercises aiming to improve strength and motor control [41-42] in reducing LBP recurrence and disability when compared to a classic approach or to no approach.

European Guidelines for chronic nonspecific LBP management recommend both supervised exercise therapy and group exercise [43]. Furthermore, literature suggests evidence for the effectiveness of exercise on pain [44] and disability [45], but limited evidence for reduction of recurrences [46].

Some strategies should be used to encourage patient adherence to exercise programs [41]. These may include monthly motivational telephone counseling or booster classes [47].

Back school is an educational and skill acquisition program, including exercises, in which all lessons are given to groups of patients under the supervision of a clinician [48].

Patient education is defined as "*a systematic experience, in a one-to-one situation, consisting of one or more methods, such as the provision of information and advice and behavior modification techniques, which influence the way the patient experiences his illness and/or his knowledge and health behavior, aimed to improving, maintaining or learning to cope with a condition* [49]". Education can include not only ergonomic advice, but also information on medication use, active coping strategies, self-efficacy beliefs, and physical activity/sport.

Multidisciplinary treatment includes multidisciplinary biopsychosocial rehabilitation with at least one physical dimension and one other dimension (psychological or social or occupational) [50]. As far as both back school and education are concerned, insufficient data confirmed their effectiveness when administered individually, but multidisciplinary treatment appeared to be moderately effective on pain intensity if compared with no treatment/waiting list controls or other treatments (exercise, physical therapy, and usual care). A group-based rehabilitation program was shown to be effective on long-term improvement in pain, disability and work participation [51].

The effectiveness of multidisciplinary treatments may be related to the combined effect of different treatments. According to van Middelkoop [45], the most promising interventions in chronic LBP are multidisciplinary treatment or behavioral treatment. Moreover, adding behavioral components can reduce the amount of sick leave.

In conclusion, multidisciplinary treatment, cognitive/behavioral treatment and exercise may be considered to be the most effective therapeutic tools for chronic LBP.

Multimodal Group Program

MGP is based on evidence of efficacy, including exercise, education and cognitive/behavioral components. It consists of ten consecutive sessions on a weekly basis performed in a spacious room within a physical therapy facility. Participants are patients previously treated with individual physical therapy interventions. Group treatment aims to provide participants with practical tools (exercise, advice, and cognitive/behavioral means) to make them active protagonists in their recovery.

The program is defined as multi-modal because exercises play a very relevant, yet not exclusive, role. Explanations on pain and ergonomic strategies are also important to promote active coping and reduce the risk and frequency of recurrences.

Given the various clinical conditions (herniated disc, arthritis, spinal stenosis, lumbar instability) and the resulting different needs in terms of exercises, components that constitute the main topic of each meeting are education to understand and manage chronic pain, ergonomic advice at home and at work, posture correction and motor control.

Education and Ergonomics

During every session, participants receive practical guidance on suggested postures and strategies to actively manage and/or relieve pain. This short program is inserted at the beginning of each session, during the warm-up phase, and is divided in two parts. The first five sessions concern education, whereas the last five ergonomics. For both parts, the first four meetings are aimed at learning, whereas the last one is dedicated to participant questions or concerns on the covered topics (see Table 1) [52].

Table 1. "Pills" of Education and Ergonomics

Education	
Meeting #1	Origin and transmission of pain
Meeting #2	Modulation of pain: descending pathways, role of drugs and exercise
Meeting #3	Active and passive coping strategies: different effects
Meeting #4	Previous lessons review, supported by Holten Institute's diagram [52] to mark the right procedure: pain → awareness → active coping → physical activity
Meeting #5	Word to patient: questions, concerns, etc.
Ergonomics	
Meeting #6	The correct sitting posture: at home, at work, driving car, with or without lumbar support
Meeting #7	The correct standing posture
Meeting #8	Loads carrying, with or without lumbar support
Meeting #9	Practical simulation of corrected postures and loads management
Meeting #10	Word to patient: questions, concerns, etc.

Posture and Motor Control

The group setting prevents the application of a "disease-specific" protocol, therefore relevant space is dedicated to generally useful training. As a consequence, postural control exercises as well as lumbo-pelvic active stabilization constitute the main contents of this protocol.

Postural control exercises aim to improve the distribution of loads and thus concern the correct position of lumbar spine and pelvis, even in relation to adjacent districts like the hips or the thoracic spine. Exercises in standing position also aim to train coordination and proprioception.

Muscle strengthening begins from awareness of the lumbar neutral zone in supine and quadruped positions, and progression incorporates the use of small tools like unstable platforms. Further progression includes selective activation of the deep abdominal muscles with relaxed breathing, co-contraction of deep abdominals and multifidus muscles, increasing the holding time, and finally adding increased loads, higher speed or further resistance.

This program is built on the basis of scientific evidence on the relevance of lumbo-pelvic motor control in the different diagnostic categories represented in our group (herniated discs, stenosis, osteoarthritis, lumbar instability) [53-56].

Organization of Sessions

Each meeting lasts one hour and is always fully organized and supervised by the same physical therapist. Each session is structured in different phases as follows: warm-up, active joint mobilization, core stability training, flexibility and stretching exercises, and finally, breathing exercises.

Warm-up - This first stage takes place in the standing position, asking participants to perform general nonspecific movements of their trunk and arms, without any tools, aiming to involve all parts of their body. Participants walk around the perimeter of a large room, first walking normally, and then modifying their walk (standing on their toes and heels, elevating their knees, crossing their legs, walking backwards, etc.). Then, while continuing to walk, participants add counter-clockwise circles with their upper arms, or self-traction by bringing their hands together above their heads. Warm-up exercises must be very simple, repetitive and easily understandable, allowing people to pay attention also to the educational concepts suggested by the physical therapist. Ergonomic advice is first given, and then simulated at the end of this phase. Overall duration of warm-up is about 10 minutes.

Active joint mobilization - Subsequently, participants perform active lumbar spine movements in the standing position, according to their flexibility. Repetitive flexion with hands on the legs, extensions with hands on the pelvis, side gliding, lateral flexion and rotation to the left and the right are performed. On a mat in the supine position, participants perform repeated hip flexion, actively assisted by their hands, lumbar flexion with both legs to the chest, lumbar lateral flexion and rotation both with raised legs and with feet resting on the ground. Moreover, anterior- posterior pelvic tilting, alternate or circling ankle movements in the supine position, and lumbar extensions in the prone position are performed. The overall duration of this second phase is about 10 minutes.

Core stability training - This is the program cornerstone, lasting 30 minutes. Exercises are organized to progressively increase in difficulty, from awareness of the neutral position of various districts (pelvis, lumbar, thoracic and cervical spine, and shoulder girdle) to motor control training in functional tasks, according to the model proposed by O'Sullivan [57].

These exercises are carried out in different positions: supine, prone, on the side, sitting and standing, in order to guarantee complete reinforcement of the "core" (transversus abdominis, multifidus, internal obliques, psoas, diaphragm, pelvic floor) and the "slings" (latissimus dorsi, thoracolumbar fascia, gluteus maximus, gluteus medius, biceps femoris, internal and external oblique, adductors). Different tools like elastic bands, light weights, sticks, medium or large unstable plates, balls, bouncers are also used for circle training (see Figures 1-10). These exercises integrate different approaches, including Pilates.

Figure 1. Active sit-up.

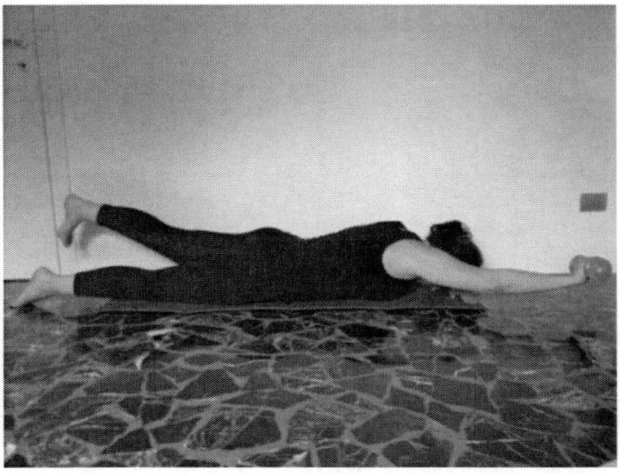

Figure 2. Extensors endurance training with light weight.

Figure 3. Extensors training in quadruped position.

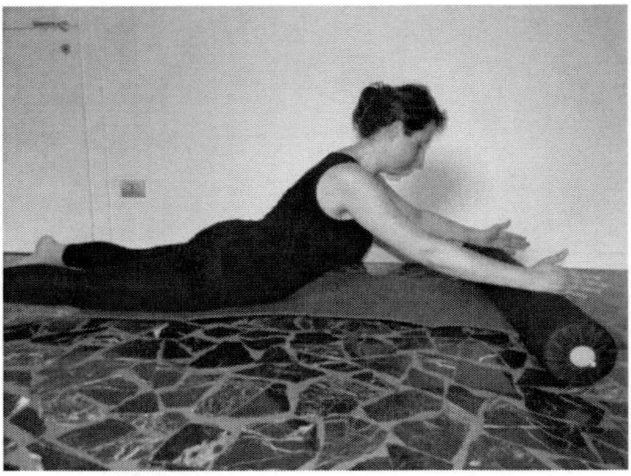

Figure 4. Extensors training.

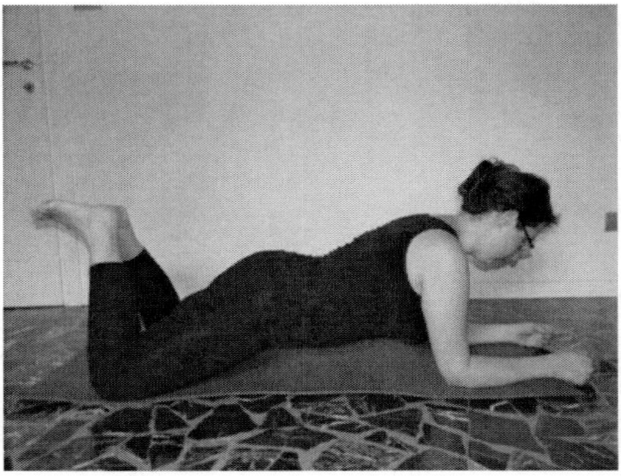

Figure 5. Prone bridge with heels squeeze.

Figure 6. Lateral bridge.

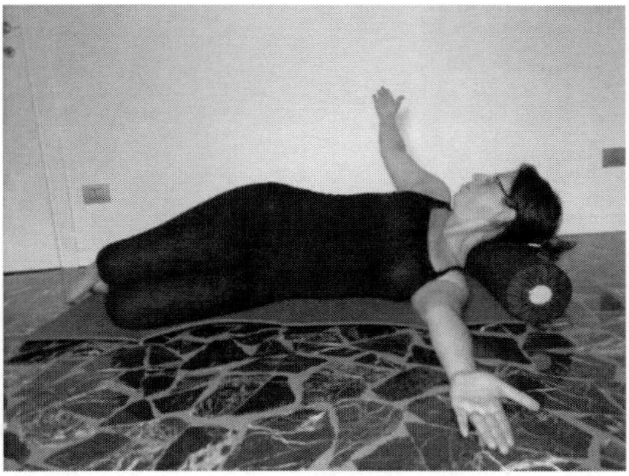

Figure 7. Spinal rotation.

Figure 8. Spinal rotation in sitting position with elastic resistance.

Figure 9. Single leg stretch.

Figure 10. Proprioceptive training on unstable platform.

Stretching and breathing exercises - The last 10 minutes of each meeting are dedicated to stretching and breathing. This choice allows patients to cool down and re-balance muscular tone. This phase begins with trunk and upper limb stretching exercises, first in dynamic and then in static mode.

Breathing is used as the last exercise and is carried out in the supine position, with legs flexed on the ground or against a wall, depending on individual needs or preferences. According to Global Postural Reeducation suggestions [58], exercises enhance the perception of different types of breathing (more diaphragmatic or more costal) to promote spine relaxation while maintaining conscious and active control on other joints. These stretching and breathing exercises, as well as some motor control procedures, are also recommended as home self-treatment to be carried out two to three times during the week.

PART FOUR - EXAMPLE OF GROUP TREATMENT

To show a Multimodal Group Program (MGP) model, a prospective observational pilot study was conducted on a small sample of subjects affected by chronic LBP, over a period of about two months, from March 24, 2014 to June 9, 2014.

Materials and Methods

Subjects

Eligible subjects were patients affected by chronic (lasting for at least 3 months) LBP who were referred to a Physical Therapy Private Practice. Exclusion criteria were cardiovascular, metabolic, neoplastic, or respiratory comorbidities, vertebral and/or spinal cord pathologies, previous spinal surgery or trauma, peripheral neuropathies and workers' compensation patients.

The following information was collected for each subject: demographic data (age and gender), education, job title, clinical characteristics such as height, weight, and lifestyle information (smoking habits), pain localization (lumbar area with or without radicular or referral symptoms), clinical diagnosis (e.g. nonspecific LBP, spondylolisthesis, lumbar stenosis, disk pathologies, osteoarthritis, lumbar instability), drugs, and comorbidities.

Intervention

MGP was similar to those proposed by Pillastrini et al. [33] and it was composed of ten weekly graded sessions for ten consecutive weeks. Each one hour session was conducted in a large room of the private practice by a physical therapist specialized in Orthopaedic Manipulative Therapy (OMT). The group was composed of 6 people.

Intervention consisted of three main components: joint, muscular and neurodynamic training, cognitive-behavioral notions to manage pain, and ergonomic advice. Exercises were aimed to improving lumbar range of motion, training the main spine stabilizers (transversus abdominis, oblique abdominal, multifidus, quadratus lumborum and erector spinae muscles [59]) and restoring physiological neurodynamics. Physical therapist encouraged subjects to perform some home exercises for ten minutes a day; these exercises were specific for each subject because of the different clinical presentations. Subject compliance was not taken into consideration as an outcome measure, but was simply encouraged. Furthermore, the physical therapist provided subjects with cognitive-behavioral notions to manage pain and guided them through a process of desensitization from fears and concerns. Physical therapist highlighted the importance of paying attention to functional activities and improving aerobic endurance. Finally, ergonomic advice on daily living and working activities was given.

Outcome Measures

To evaluate physical disability and pain, Oswestry Disability Questionnaire in its Italian version (ODI-I) [60], Roland & Morris Disability Questionnaire (RMDQ) [61] and Numerical Rating Scale (NRS) [62] were used. To evaluate some psychological and cognitive aspects related to chronic pain, Tampa Scale of Kinesiophobia (TSK) in its Italian version [63] was administered. Finally, perceived health status was investigated using the Italian version of the Short-Form Health Survey Questionnaire (SF-36) [64].

ODI-I is a self-administered questionnaire composed of ten sections in which higher levels of disability correspond to higher score percentage. The first section rates pain intensity and the others describe its disabling effect on typical daily activities. The score for each item ranges from 0 to 5, and the sum of the ten scores is expressed as a percentage of the maximum score and thus ranges from 0 (no disability) to 100 (maximum disability). ODI-I has proven to be reliable, valid and sensitive to change [65]. According to proposed cut-off values for minimal important change of frequently used functional status measures in LBP [66], a 30% change from baseline was considered a clinically meaningful improvement for the ODI-I.

Roland and Morris Disability Questionnaire (RMDQ) is a self-administered tool. It is useful to investigate especially mild to severe disability due to LBP. RMDQ is very simple to fill in as the patient simply needs to tick the statements describing his/her current condition. The score is calculated by summing the ticked boxes and ranges from 0 (no disability) to 24 (maximum disability). The Minimal Clinically Important Difference (MCID) for all types of LBP, both acute and chronic, corresponds to 3.5 points [67].

Evaluation of lumbar physical discomfort was recorded with a self-reported NRS [62]. NRS scores range from 0 (no pain) to 10 (the worst possible pain) and its MCID is estimated to be 30% change from baseline [66].

TSK focuses on thoughts in relation to pain and exercises, but not to work situations. It is composed of 17 items, 13 of which aim to evaluate fear of movement and lesions. The total score ranges from 13 to 52 points [63]. A score ≥37 is considered clinically significant. Unfortunately, we have no indications from literature on the MCID of this questionnaire.

Quality of life was assessed using SF-36 and the domain scores were calculated on the basis of the User Manual for the Italian version [68]. For SF-36 the MCID was achieved when 30% increases were shown [69].

All scales were applied before starting the treatment (baseline time, T0) and at the end of the treatment period (follow-up, T1). Outcome measurements were collected by the same physical therapists involved in treatment.

Data Analysis

Anthropometric and clinical characteristics and outcome measures at baseline were shown via descriptive statistics. Analyses were carried out for the short-term differences in disability, pain and psychological scores from baseline.

In order to evaluate the statistical significance of the reduction in disability, pain, fear of movement and the improvement in perceived health status, Student's t-test was performed on ODI, NRS, TSK and SF-36 score differences from baseline. Variations in scale scores were reported in absolute values. The significance level was set at 95%.

Results

Anthropometric and clinical characteristics of the group are shown in Table 2. Outcome measures at baseline and immediately after the treatment are reported in Table 3. From an observational point of view, the immediately after treatment follow-up showed an improvement in all domains (pain, disability, and fear of movement) even if none of them resulted statistically or clinically significant. Student's T test scores were respectively: ODI (P-value=0.06), RMDQ (P-value=0.15), NRS (P-value=0.07), and TSK (P-value=0.08).

Table 2. Characteristics of the sample

Variable	Category	N
Gender	F	6
	M	0
Age	< 50	2
	51-60	2
	61-70	2
Married	Yes	5
	No	1
Working	Yes	4
	No	0
	Retired	2
Education	Mid school	0
	Upper school	4
	University	2
Smoking	Yes	1
	No	5
Duration of pain	< 6 months	2
	6 months – 1 year	2
	>1 year	2
Radicular pain	Yes	3
	No	3
Drugs assumption	Yes	3
	No	3
Comorbidities	Yes	3
	No	3

Table 3. Differences in outcome measures from Time 1 and Time 0 and their statistically significance

	Time 0	Time 1	MD (Mean Difference)	P-value (Student's T test)
ODI	9.7	7.8	-1.9	0.065
RMDQ	6	4.2	-1.8	0.151
NRS	34.2	25.2	-9	0.073
TSK	29.6	27.2	-2.4	0.083
SF-36 (total score)	93.8	105.6	+11.8	0.019

ODI = Oswestry Disability Questionnaire.
RMDQ = Roland & Morris Disability Questionnaire.
NRS = Numerical Rating Scale.
TSK = Tampa Scale for Kinesiophobia.
SF-36 = Short-Form Health Survey Questionnaire.

The best result was shown on the SF-36 questionnaire, both on the total score (P-value=0.01) and the subscale "emotional state" (P-value=0.01); furthermore, the result on the "mental health" subscale was borderline (P-value=0.05).

Discussion

This pilot study showed that an MGP conducted in a physical therapy private practice can slightly reduce pain, disability and fear of movement in subjects suffering from chronic LBP in the short term. Improvements in self-perceived quality of life, especially concerning psychosocial components, appeared to be more significant.

Improvement was observed in each questionnaire and in all subjects, albeit not relevant enough to be considered statistically or clinically significant. Nevertheless, these results must be considered in light of the very small sample size involved in this pilot study.

In conclusion, an MGP combining exercises, education and cognitive-behavioral notions may be a viable, economical option to treat patients suffering from chronic LBP.

References

[1] Waxman R, Tennant A, Helliwell P. A prospective follow-up study of low back pain in the community. *Spine* 2000;25(16):2085-90.

[2] Pillastrini P, Gardenghi I, Bonetti F, Capra F, Guccione A, Mugnai R, Violante FS. An updated overview of clinical guidelines for chronic low back pain management in primary care. *Joint Bone Spine.* 2012;79(2):176-85.

[3] Hoy D, Brooks P, Blyth F, Buchbinder R. The Epidemiology of low back pain. *Best Pract. Res. Clin. Rheumatol.* 2010;24(6):769-81.

[4] Stanton TR, Latimer J, Maher CG, Hancock M. How do we define the condition 'recurrent low back pain'? A systematic review. *Eur. Spine J.* 2010;19(4):533-539.

[5] Leboeuf-Yde C, Lemeunier N, Wedderkopp N, Kjaer P. Evidence-based classification of low back pain in the general population: one-year data collected with SMS Track. *Chiropr Man Therap.* 2013;2:21:30.

[6] Itz CJ, Geurts JW, van Kleef M, Nelemans P. Clinical course of non-specific low back pain: a systematic review of prospective cohort studies set in primary care. *Eur. J. Pain.* 2013;17(1):5-15.

[7] Stanton TR, Latimer J, Maher CG, Hancock M. Definitions of recurrence of an episode of low back pain: a systematic review. *Spine* 2009;34(9):E316-22.

[8] Mannion RJ, Woolf CJ. Pain mechanisms and management: a central perspective. *The Clinical Journal of Pain*, 2000;16(3 Suppl):S144-56.

[9] Apkarian AV, Baliki MN, Geha PY. Towards a theory of chronic pain. *Progress in Neurobiology* 2009;87:81-97.

[10] Woolf CJ. Central sensitization: implications for the diagnosis and treatment of pain. *Pain* 2011;152(3 Suppl):S2-15.

[11] Smart KM, Blake C, Staines A, Thacker M, Doody C. Mechanisms-based classifications of musculoskeletal pain: part 1 of 3: symptoms and signs of central sensitisation in patients with low back (± leg) pain. *Man Ther.* 2012;17(4):336-44.

[12] Wertli MM, Rasmussen-Barr E, Weiser S, Bachmann LM, Brunner F. The role of fear avoidance beliefs as a prognostic factor for outcome in patients with nonspecific low back pain: a systematic review. *The Spine Journal* 2014;14(5):816-836.e4.

[13] Carty J, O'Donnell M, Evans L, Kazantzis N, Creamer M. Predicting posttraumatic stress disorder symptoms and pain intensity following severe injury: the role of catastrophizing. *Eur. J. Psychotraumatol.* 2011;2. Epub 2011 Apr 29.

[14] Swinkels-Meewisse IE, Roelofs J, Schouten EG, Verbeek AL, Oostendorp RA, Vlaeyen JW. Fear of movement/ (re) injury*Spine* 2006;31(6):658-64.

[15] Bekkering GE, Hendriks HJM, Koes BW, Oostendorp RAB, Ostelo RWJG, Thomassen JMC, van Tulder MW. Dutch physiotherapy guidelines for low back pain. *Physiotherapy* 2003;89:82–96.

[16] Beck, J., 1995. Cognitive Therapy: Basics and Beyond. Guildford Press: New York.

[17] Medina-Mirapeix F, Escolar-Reina P, Gascón-Cánovas JJ, Montilla-Herrador J, Collins SM. Personal characteristics influencing patients' adherence to home exercise during chronic pain: a qualitative study. *J. Rehabil. Med.* 2009;41(5):347-52.

[18] Turner JA, Jensen MP. Efficacy of cognitive therapy for chronic low back pain. *Pain* 1993;52(2):169-77.

[19] Jacobson, E. Progressive relaxation (2nd ed.). Oxford, England: Univ. Chicago Press. (1938)

[20] Rundell SD, Davenport TE. Patient education based on principles of cognitive behavioral therapy for a patient with persistent low back pain: a case report. *J. Orthop. Sports Phys. Ther.* 2010;40(8):494-501.

[21] George SZ, Zeppieri G Physical therapy utilization of graded exposure for patients with low back pain. *J. Orthop. Sports Phys. Ther.* 2009;39(7):496-505.

[22] Rasmussen-Barr E, Ang B, Arvidsson I, Nilsson-Wikmar L. Graded exercise for recurrent low-back pain: a randomized, controlled trial with 6-, 12-, and 36-month follow-ups. *Spine* 2009;34(3):221-8.

[23] Lindström I, Ohlund C, Eek C, Wallin L, Peterson LE, Nachemson A. Mobility, strength, and fitness after a graded activity program for patients with subacute low back pain. A randomized prospective clinical study with a behavioral therapy approach. *Spine* 1992;17(6):641-52.

[24] Escolar-Reina P, Medina-Mirapeix F, Gascón-Cánovas JJ, Montilla-Herrador J, Jimeno-Serrano FJ, de Oliveira Sousa SL, del Baño-Aledo ME, Lomas-Vega R. How do care-provider and home exercise program characteristics affect patient adherence in chronic neck and back pain: a qualitative study. *BMC Health Serv Res*. 2010;10(10):60.

[25] Cooper K, Smith BH, Hancock E. Patients' perception of self-management of chronic low back pain: evidence for enhancing patients education and support. *Physiotherapy*, 2009;95(1):43-50.

[26] Henschke N, Ostelo RW, van Tulder MW, Vlaeyen JW, Morley S, Assendelft WJ, Main CJ. Behavioural treatment*Cochrane Database Syst. Rev*. 2010 Jul 7;(7):CD002014.

[27] van Middelkoop M, Rubinstein SM, Kuijpers T, Verhagen AP, Ostelo R, Koes BW, van Tulder MW. A systematic review on the effectiveness of physical and rehabilitation interventions for chronic non-specific low back pain. *Eur. Spine J*. 2011;20(1):19-39.

[28] Macedo LG, Smeets RJ, Maher CG, Latimer J, McAuley JH. Graded activity and graded exposure for persistent nonspecific low back pain: a systematic review. *Phys. Ther*. 2010;90(6):860-79.

[29] George SZ, Wittmer VT, Fillingim RB, Robinson ME. Comparison of graded exercise and graded exposure clinical outcomes for patients with chronic low back pain. *J. Orthop. Sports Phys. Ther*. 2010;40(11):694-704.

[30] Mirza SK, Deyo RA Systematic Review of Randomized Trials Comparing Lumbar Fusion Surgery to Nonoperative Care for Treatment of Chronic Back Pain. *Spine* 2007;32(7):816-823.

[31] Santandrea S, Boschi M, Vanti C. Efficacy of Cognitive Behavioural Therapy in non-specific neck pain: a systematic review. (Italian) *Scienza Riabilitativa* 2011;13(2):5-23.

[32] Frank JW, Bair MJ, Becker WC, Krebs EE, Liebschutz JM, Alford DP. Update in Pain Medicine for Primary Care Providers: A Narrative Review, 2010–2012. *Pain Medicine*, 2014;15(3):425-31.

[33] Pillastrini P, Bonfiglioli R, Banchelli F, Capra F, Resende Fde L, Villafane JH, Vanti C, Violante FS. The effect of a multimodal group programme in hospital workers with persistent low back pain: a prospective observational study. *Med. Lav.* 2013; 104(5):380-92.

[34] van Tulder MW, Koes BW, Metsemakers JF, Bouter LM. Chronic low back pain in primary care: a prospective study on the management and course. *Fam. Pract.* 1998;15(2):126-32.

[35] Grotle M, Foster NE, Dunn KM, Croft P. Are prognostic indicators for poor outcome different for acute and chronic low back pain consulters in primary care? *Pain* 2010;151(3):790-7.

[36] Steffens D, Hancock MJ, Maher CG, Latimer J, Satchell R, Ferreira M, Ferreira PH, Partington M, Bouvier AL. Prognosis of chronic low back pain in patients presenting to a private community-based group exercise program. *Eur. Spine J.* 2014;23(1):113-9.

[37] Abenhaim L, Rossignol M, Valat JP, Nordin M, Avouac B, Blotman F, Charlot J, Dreiser RL, Legrand E, Rozenberg S, Vautravers P. The role of activity in the therapeutic management of back pain. Report of the International Paris Task Force on Back Pain. *Spine* 2000;25:1S–33S.

[38] Delitto A. Research in low back pain: time to stop seeking the elusive "magic bullet". *Phys. Ther* 2005;85:206-8.

[39] Larsen K, Weidick F, Leboeuf-Yde C. Can passive prone extension of the back prevent back problems? A randomized, controlled intervention trial of 314 military conscripts. *Spine* 2002;27:2747-52.

[40] Machado LA, de Souza MS, Ferreira PH, Ferreira ML. The McKenzie method for low back pain: a systematic review of the literature with a meta-analysis approach. *Spine* 2006;31:E254-62.

[41] Hayden JA, van Tulder MW, Tomlinson G. Systematic review: strategies for using exercise therapy to improve outcomes in chronic low back pain. *Ann. Intern Med.* 2005;142:776-85.

[42] Hides JA, Jull GA, Richardson CA. Long-term effects of specific stabilizing exercises for first-episode low back pain. *Spine* 2001;26:E243-8.

[43] Airaksinen O, Brox JI, Cedraschi C, Hildebrandt J, Klaber-Moffett J, Kovacs F, Mannion AF, Reis S, Staal JB, Ursin H, Zanoli G; COST B13 Working Group on Guidelines for Chronic Low Back Pain. Chapter 4. European guidelines for the management of chronic nonspecific low back pain. *Eur. Spine J.* 2006;15 Suppl 2:S192-300.

[44] Hayden JA, van Tulder MW, Malmivaara A, Koes BW. Exercise therapy for treatment of non-specific low back pain. *Cochrane Database Syst Rev*. 2005;(3):CD000335.

[45] van Middelkoop M, Rubinstein SM, Kuijpers T, Verhagen AP, Ostelo R, Koes BW, van Tulder MW. A systematic review on the effectiveness of physical and rehabilitation interventions for chronic non-specific low back pain. *Eur. Spine J.* 2011; 20(1):19-39.

[46] Bell JA, Burnett A. Exercise for the primary, secondary and tertiary prevention of low back pain in the workplace: a systematic review. *J. Occup. Rehabil.* 2009;19(1):8-24).

[47] Tavafian SS, Jamshidi AR, Mohammad K. Treatment of low back pain: randomized clinical trial comparing a multidisciplinary group-based rehabilitation program with oral drug treatment up to 12 months. *Int. J. Rheum. Dis.* 2014;17(2):159-64.

[48] Heymans MW, van Tulder MW, Esmail R, Bombardier C, Koes BW. Back schools for non-specific low-back pain. *Cochrane Database Syst. Rev.* 2004:CD000261.

[49] Engers A, Jellema P, Wensing M, van der Windt DA, Grol R, van Tulder MW. Individual patient education for low back pain. *Cochrane Database Syst.* 2008 Rev:CD004057.

[50] Guzman J, Esmail R, Karjalainen K, Malmivaara A, Irvin E, Bombardier C. Multidisciplinary rehabilitation for chronic low back pain: systematic review. *BMJ* 2001;322:1511–1516.

[51] Dufour N, Thamsborg G, Oefeldt A, Lundsgaard C, Stender S. Treatment of chronic low back pain: a randomized, clinical trial comparing group-based multidisciplinary biopsychosocial rehabilitation and intensive individual therapist-assisted back muscle strengthening exercises. *Spine* 2010;35(5):469-76.

[52] Torstensen TA. The Mirror book. Holten Institute AB. Lidingo, Sweden.

[53] Macedo LG1, Latimer J, Maher CG, Hodges PW, McAuley JH, Nicholas MK, Tonkin L, Stanton CJ, Stanton TR, Stafford R. Effect of

motor control exercises versus graded activity in patients with chronic nonspecific low back pain: a randomized controlled trial. *Phys. Ther.* 2012;92(3):363-77.

[54] Comerford MJ, Mottram SL. Functional stability re-training: principles and strategies for managing mechanical dysfunction. *Man. Ther.* 2001;6(1):3-14.

[55] Bodack M, O'Sullivan PB, Twomey LT, Allison GT. Evaluation of specific stabilizing exercise in the treatment of chronic low back pain with radiologic diagnosis of spondylolysis or spondylolisthesis. *Spine* 1997; 22(24):2959-67.

[56] Monteiro M. Therapeutic exercise in the treatment of patients with lumbar spinal stenosis. *Clin. Orthop Relat. Res*. 2001;(384):144-52.

[57] O'Sullivan PB. Lumbar segmental instability: clinical presentation and specific stabilizing exercise management. *Manual Therapy* 2000, 5(1):2-12.

[58] Bonetti F, Curti S, Mattioli S, Mugnai R, Vanti C, Violante FS, Pillastrini P. Effectiveness of a 'Global Postural Reeducation' program for persistent Low Back Pain: a non-randomised controlled trial. *BMC Musculoskeletal Disorders* 2010,11:285.

[59] Pillastrini P, Mugnai R, Bertozzi L, Costi S, Curti S, Mattioli S, Violante FS. Effectiveness of an at-work exercise program in the prevention and management of neck and low back complaints in nursery school teachers. *Ind. Health* 2009;47:349-54.

[60] Monticone M, Baiardi P, Ferrari S, Foti C, Mugnai R, Pillastrini P, Vanti C, Zanoli G. Development of the Italian version of the Oswestry Disability Index (ODI-I): A cross cultural adaptation, reliability and validity study. *Spine* 2009; 34(19):2090-5.

[61] Roland M, Fairbank J. The Roland and Morris Disability Questionnaire and the Oswestry Disability Index. *Spine* 2000;25(24):3115-24.

[62] Childs JD, Piva SR, Fritz JM. Responsiveness of the Numeric Pain Rating Scale in patients with low back pain. *Spine* 2005; 30:1331–1334.

[63] Monticone M, Giorgi I, Baiardi P, Barbieri M, Rocca B, Bonezzi C. Development of the Italian version of the Tampa Scale of Kinesiophobia (TSK-I): cross-cultural adaptation, factor analysis, reliability, and validity. *Spine* 2010; 35(12):1241-6.

[64] Apolone G, Mosconi P. The Italian SF-36 Survey: translation, validation and norming. *J. Clin. Epidemiol.* 1998;51(11):1025-36.

[65] Monticone M, Baiardi P, Vanti C, Ferrari S, Pillastrini P, Mugnai R, Foti C. Responsiveness of the Oswestry Disability Index and the Roland

Morris Disability Questionnaire in Italian subjects with sub-acute and chronic low back pain. *Eur. Spine J.* 2012; 21(1):122-9.

[66] Ostelo RW, Deyo RA, Stratford P. Interpreting change scores for pain and functional status in low back pain: towards international consensus regarding minimal important change. *Spine* 2008;33, 90–4.

[67] Ostelo RW, DeVet HC. Clinically important outcomes in low back pain. *Best Pract. Res. Clin. Rheumat.* 2005;19(4):593-607.

[68] Apolone G, Mosconi P, Ware J. Questionario sullo stato di salute SF-36. Manuale d'uso e guida all'interpretazione dei risultati. [SF-36 Quality of Life Questionnaire. User's Manual and Guide to the Interpretation of Results]. 2000 Guerini e Associati Editors, Milan (in Italian).

[69] Spratt KF. Patient-level minimal clinically important difference based on clinical judgment and minimally detectable measurement difference: a rationale for the SF-36 physical function scale in the SPORT intervertebral disc herniation cohort. *Spine* 2009;34(16):1722-3.

In: Group Therapy
Editor: Hellen Derrickson
ISBN: 978-1-63463-173-0

Chapter 5

PSYCHOLOGICAL EFFECTS OF COLLABORATIVE LEGO® BLOCK CREATION

Daiki Kato
Kinjo Gakuin University, Nagoya, Japan

ABSTRACT

In this chapter, I overviewed the application of collaborative LEGO® block creation and examined its psychological effects. First, previous studies concerned with collaborative LEGO® block creation were reviewed.

Secondly the effect of the creation, especially in social skills and trust, was examined. Third, the effect of the collaborative creation, in the sense of being accepted by others, was also examined. These results indicate that collaborative work facilitates social skills and the division of roles, positively affecting the sense of acceptance, and presenting a new possibility for the application of block creation in the field of group therapy. Finally, we introduced the practices of collaborative LEGO® block creation based on these studies. This group work is also effective for children with developmental disorders, such as autism, and groups requiring cross-cultural communication.

Introduction

Block Creation in Individual Psychotherapy

Toy blocks were originally developed as a playing tool for children. They are small blocks of plastic in different colors. Over the years, adolescents and adults have also started to enjoy playing with blocks in certain contexts. Although blocks were originally developed as toys, they are used in several other fields such as the arts, education, and technology. In the area of psychology, some studies have been conducted to see how playing with blocks influences children's cognitive development. In the field of psychotherapy, Resnick (1976) published the study entitled "Block Playing as a Therapeutic Technique." In this study, Playskool blocks, one of the many different brands of toy blocks, were used as materials. The blocks served as a medium for couples and families to communicate with each other. While one participant expressed something using blocks, the other participant was made to restructure the expression, using blocks, based on information received from their partners. The partners alternated roles throughout the sessions and this process helped facilitate their communication. This study was seen as pioneering for its application of block creation in psychotherapy. Another attempt to use block creation in psychotherapy was seen in a session with a mute child. In Irie and Omori (1991), the child used the blocks as a means of communication with the therapist. The child's expressions gradually increased in both content and creativity, which reduced the symptoms of the mutism. Imagawa et al. (1985) compared the use of blocks as a medium of expression to conventional psychotherapy for patients diagnosed with schizophrenia, and the results indicated that the former had a more positive impact than the latter.

Based on a study examining the use of blocks in art therapy, Kato (2006) developed an expressive technique using blocks (Block Technique) and studied its effects. This new technique was based on both sand play therapy and the use of collage therapy (which is quite popular in Japan). Sand play therapy was developed by Kalff (1966), where participants described their mental imagery by using several toy figures in a box filled with sand. Collage therapy was originally developed as an artistic technique but it also provides useful material for art therapy. In this type of therapy, patients cut pictures out of magazines or advertisements and paste them on drawing paper. Both of these techniques (sand play and collage) provide a secure framework for conducting therapy, a very important feature in the field of psychotherapy. For the block technique, we provided LEGO® blocks for each participant, including basic cubic blocks and specially-shaped blocks representing plants, animals, and figures. To begin, the clients were instructed to express anything they wanted using the blocks on a green colored base plate (25 cm × 25 cm). Kato (2006) examined the technique's psychological effects by using the Profile of Mood States (POMS), which is a multi-disciplinary questionnaire that evaluates participants' moods. In this study, participants were asked to complete the POMS as a pre-test followed by the free block play task. Finally, they completed the POMS as a post-test and the results of the three tests were compared. The scores on the POMS after the completion of the block task were significantly lower on the Tension-Anxiety, Depression-Dejection, Anger-Hostility, Fatigue-Inertia, and the Confusion-Bewilderment scales. These results indicated that the LEGO® block task may have had a positive therapeutic effect on the moods of the participants.

Block Creation in Groups

Block creation has also been found to be useful in group therapy settings. It has been found to be a very effective medium for both facilitating communication and for helping participants understand each other in different types of groups. The application of this technique in different settings is why several different variations of it have been developed and practiced over the years. I will describe some of them later in this section.

The LEGO® Serious Play (LSP) exercise is popular in the business world as a means of facilitating effective communication. The original concept was developed by Roos and Victor (1998, 1999). Participants complete tasks by building symbolic and metaphorical models with LEGO® blocks and they then present them to the other participants. In the first step of LSP, the facilitator assigns a task to the participants and they build their answers using LEGO® blocks. Then, each group presents their own story based on their block creations to the other groups. Through the workshop, the different thought patterns of each member become apparent, which makes it easier for them to communicate and understand each other. Therefore, this process could be beneficial for both companies and organizations trying to improve their employees' communication skills.

The other approach, which is known as a "Story Starter," is a collaborative approach used in the field of education. Students are encouraged to express themselves by using blocks and figures and to then take photos of the end products. These pictures are then uploaded onto a computer so the students can add decorations and comments to them. Students then match their own original stories with the pictures and share them. This method is expected to enhance students' communication and presentation skills. The method is also used in the education of language, information technology, etc.

Another approach to the application of toy blocks is group therapy. LeGoff (2004) developed a social skills training program for children with autism spectrum disorders (ASD). ASD is one of the core symptoms of developmental disorders. According to DSM-5, one of the main features of ASD is the persistent deficit in both social communication and interaction. Another trait is restricted and repetitive patterns of behavior, interests, or activities. When it comes to deficient social skills, collaborative block creation has been found to be very effective. The approach used by LeGoff is called "LEGO® Therapy" and it has been used extensively in groups with children diagnosed with ASD. The participants are assigned roles such as "engineer," "supplier," and "builder," and they are encouraged to work together in order to solve a particular task. The engineer is told to give instructions to the other group members. The supplier is in charge of choosing appropriate blocks and providing them to the group. Lastly, the builder follows instructions and constructs the figures. The efficient collaboration and division of the roles facilitates both verbal and non-verbal communication. In addition, the participants are more likely to share their creativity and problem solving skills with others throughout the process, which enhances their social skills. Based on previous findings with LEGO® Therapy, Owens et al. (2008) tested the method with a group of children diagnosed with ASD. They also included the Social Use of Language Program (SULP) as a tool for social skills training. They evaluated the different results of the groups and found that the LEGO® Therapy group's social skills improved more than the others' did. They also found that maladaptive behaviors significantly decreased more in both the LEGO® Therapy and SULP groups compared to the control group.

The Block Technique has also been used in group therapy settings. As shown in the previous section, the technique was originally developed to be a tool for individual psychotherapy. Based on the structures of both sand play and collage therapy, the clients expressed anything that comes to mind on the plate by using blocks and figures. The therapists observed the creative process and they noted that it had some therapeutic effects. This framework was also found to be useful in group therapy. In our study, we used this technique with groups and divided the participants into groups of three to five. The facilitator observed each group and watched over the emotional expression process. At first, we provided a green LEGO® plate (which combined four pieces of 25cm

× 25cm plates) for the group expression task. Then, the facilitator instructed them to create anything they wanted while collaborating with the other group members. After the task was completed, the members and the facilitator discussed why they chose to express themselves the way they did. This technique was effective in the group setting, although it was originally developed as a medium for individual psychotherapy and art therapy. In view of this positive outcome, we decided to use this method with a group of international students that were already receiving student counseling and with a group of children that had previously been diagnosed with developmental disorders such as ASD or ADHD. The details of the outcomes of the two groups are described in the further section.

I have already described several group approaches that used blocks as a medium for communication. I would now like to describe the different features used with each approach. The different categories for the group approaches that used block creations are shown in Figure 1.

The horizontal axis represents the different ages of the participants. In contrast, the vertical axis shows the different structures of the techniques. For instance, LEGO® Therapy and LEGO® Serious Play are the most structured techniques according to the figure. This means that their evidence, materials, and procedures were very structured.

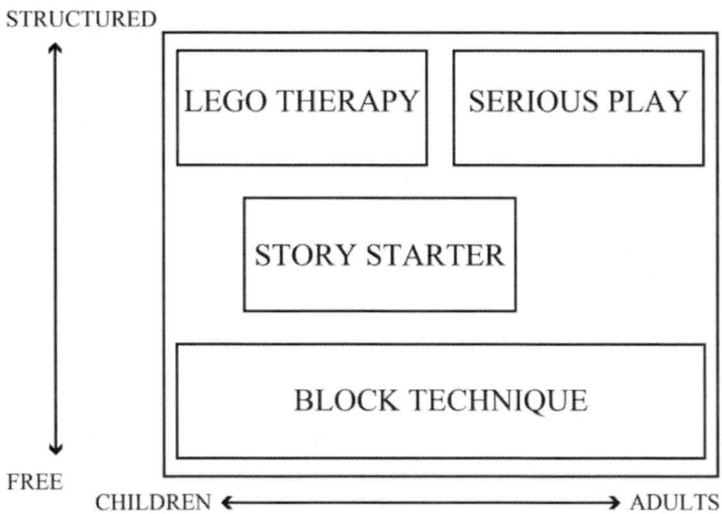

Figure 1. Categories of the group approaches using block creation.

Their objectives are also very clear: LEGO® Therapy was developed to help children with ASD build proper social skills, and LEGO® Serious Play was developed to facilitate both communication and productivity within companies and organizations. LEGO® Therapy was designed to be used with children, while LEGO® Serious Play was developed to be used with adults. Figure 1 depicts Story Starter as a semi-structured technique, which means it has a fair amount of structure while also providing some opportunities for free expression. However, although LEGO® is used as the material and standard guidelines already exist for teachers who use Story Starter, they can still change the details based on their preferred objectives and varying situations. This flexibility suits the needs of the field of education and makes it easier to apply in different countries. Block Technique is a more subjective approach than all the others. Of course, this does not mean that it is structure-free; it still requires specific group sizes, plates, and the presence of a facilitator. This increased freedom of expression in Block Technique encourages the participants to describe some of their unconscious imagery, which is why it has been found to have therapeutic effects. The details about the psychological effects of Block Technique will be discussed in greater detail in the next section.

EFFECTS OF COLLABORATIVE BLOCK CREATION ON SOCIAL SKILLS AND TRUST

In this study, we examined the effects of collaborative block creation from the viewpoints of social skills and trust. The evidence is based on Kato et al. (2012). We focused on the psychological aspects of social skills, trust in others, and trust in oneself that were examined during the activity. The participants were high school students and our hypothesis proposed that social skills, trust in others, and trust in oneself would significantly increase through collaborative expression through block creation.

Method

Participants

Thirty-nine Japanese high school students participated in this study (six males and 33 females; all participants were either 16 or 17 years old). The collaborative expression activity was conducted as part of a psychology class in a university summer school. The participants were randomly divided into groups of three or four.

Materials

LEGO®'s green plastic plates (50cm × 50cm) and several types of blocks were provided for each group. The basic blocks provided were standard cube-shaped blocks with the following colors: red, blue, green, yellow, white, black, and brown. We also provided a variety of differently shaped blocks such as animals, plants, wheels, windows, and doors. LEGO® sets usually contain human figures and so, a number of male and female figures were given to each group. The human figures came with uniforms, clothes, tools, and bags that correspond with a variety of occupations such as office workers, carpenters, and police officers.

Procedure

The participants were asked to express themselves collaboratively with the other group members, and they were encouraged to build anything they wanted on the group's plate using LEGO® blocks and figures. They were also asked to complete two questionnaires about their social skills and trust before and after the activity. For this part, we used the 18-item Kikuchi Scale of Social Skills (KiSS-18; Kikuchi, 1988), which is a scale used to measure a participant's general social skills with a one-factor model. Items on this scale include: "I can join in conversation with others smoothly" and "I can express my feeling to others." We also used a scale developed by Amagai (1995) to measure trust. It includes 24 items that are partitioned into three different factors: trust for others, trust in oneself, and distrust. In this study, we only used the trust for others (six items) and trust in oneself (eight items) factors. Both scales have been widely used in studies in Japan and their reliability and validity have previously been examined by other researchers. Therefore, we only used the original items and factors for these scales in this study.

Results and Discussion

The scores for social skills, trust in others, and trust in oneself before and after the collaborative expression stage were compared using paired t-tests. They revealed that the questionnaire scores before and after the activity for social skills ($t(38) = -4.16$, $p < .01$) and trust in others ($t(38) = -2.28$, $p < .05$) were significantly higher after the activity than before it. However, the difference in trust in oneself before and after the activity was not significant ($t(38) = -0.48$, *n.s.*).

The research hypothesis for this study was partially supported by the results. Although the scores for social skills and trust in others increased, the scores for trust in oneself remained unchanged. Participants' social skills significantly increased through the experience of collaborative expression. Although many of the participants were meeting each other for the first time, they had no problems communicating by using blocks as a medium. Effective social skills are important for forming positive relationships with others and in this study; the experience of collaborative expression had a positive effect on the participants' abilities.

Being able to join in conversations and express feelings to others, which are both social skills measured by the KiSS-18 (Kikuchi, 1988), are very important in interpersonal communication. Sometimes, it may be difficult for people to use these skills appropriately in a new situation or when meeting a person for the first time. Moreover, certain participants may be nervous or anxious before the collaborative expression. For people to employ social skills effectively, they need to adapt to the group and its other members. Kato (2006) showed that play block expression significantly reduces tension and anxiety in group settings, which helps the participants relax, adapt to the group, and increase their social skills.

Trusting other people in the group was found to significantly increase after the activity. We assume that the participants were interested in meeting all the other members of their group and came to know each other through the collaboration exercise. As a result of the facilitation of positive regard for others through collaborative expression and conversation, the participants' trust in others increased after completing the activity. In contrast, the scores for trust in oneself were not significantly changed through the completion of the activity. Trust in oneself is a personal, psychological construct and is strongly connected to the foundation of one's personality. It cannot be changed in the short term because a significant increase in it requires engagement in continuous introspection. As with the theory of art therapy or counseling, a continuous therapeutic process is sometimes necessary to facilitate insight into oneself. In this study, the collaborative expression was the first and only opportunity for participants to engage in this activity. Future research should examine the effects of block creation over a period of time to investigate additional clinical applications. Also, in order to expand the range of applications for the collaborative block creation, practical and statistical studies, which would include several types of participants and psychological aspects, would need to be conducted.

The results obtained in this study showed that collaborative block creation had positive effects on the participants' social skills and trust in others, and could be used in education, therapy, and cross-cultural group settings as a medium for communication. In future studies, the multiple effects of this method should be examined.

EFFECTS OF COLLABORATIVE BLOCK CREATION ON THE SENSE OF ACCEPTANCE

In this study, we examined the effect of collaborative block creation from the viewpoint of the sense of being accepted by others. The evidence is based on Kato et al. (2013a). Psychologists have previously investigated the effects of group cooperation and cohesion. For example, Turner et al. (1987) developed the self-categorization theory and predicted that working in a group could enhance people's social identities, which would result in reciprocal positive evaluations, trust among group members, and would also enhance the individual's sense of acceptance by others. Yli-Piipari et al. (2011) examined the roles of peer groups and gender in regard to adolescents' task values and physical activity and found that the effect of group dynamics on adolescents was an important research theme. Their results indicated that the feeling of peer group membership was a significant determinant of future activity. The study in the previous section found that when high school students constructed a collaborative block creation together, it significantly increased their social skills and trust of others.

The term "Ibasho" is an important term in Japanese adolescent psychology that translates literally as "whereabouts" or "a place of my own." Ishimoto (2010) defined Ibasho as the sense of being accepted by others unconditionally. Norisada (2008) defined the term by describing four important factors regarding adolescent communication: sense of authenticity, sense of role, sense of perceived acceptance, and sense of relief. In addition, adolescents' friendship styles are also an important part of Ibasho. For example, Ishimoto et al. (2009) found that respectful friendships resulted in improved social and psychological adjustment at school for Japanese female adolescents. Since Ibasho is concerned with the cognition of an individual's relationship with others and his/her friendship styles, we reasoned that an individual's experience of engaging in a collaborative task would help the development of Ibasho. In order to prove our theory, our study seeks to determine the effect that constructing a collaborative LEGO® block creation would have on the Ibasho of young Japanese women in late adolescence.

Method

Participants

Participants in this study were 20 female undergraduate students at a Japanese women-only university (M = 20.15 years, SD = 0.37). We should note here that although women in this age group would be considered young adults in some other countries of the world, most of the participants would be identified within the period of late adolescence in Japan. All of the participants were volunteers who were taking a clinical psychology course that focused on psychotherapy methods, art therapy, and different group therapy approaches. The collaborative LEGO® block construction activity was held over two class periods. There were nine participants in the first class and eleven in the second, and the students were randomly divided into groups of either three or four.

Materials and Procedure

We provided green LEGO® plastic building plates (50 cm^2) and several types of blocks to each group, the same as described in the previous section. We asked the participants to work with the other members of their groups in order to create any formation or construction they imagined on the building plate using both LEGO® blocks and figures. In addition, the participants were asked to complete their structures within 60 minutes and to answer all of the surveys regarding their Ibasho before and after the activity. We used the Sense of Ibasho Scale (Asai, 2013), which is based on Norisada's Sense of Ibasho Scale for Adolescents (2008). Norisada's scale consists of four subscales: sense of authenticity, sense of role, sense of perceived acceptance, and sense of relief. Respondents that completed Norisada's scale were required to imagine a specific person (e.g., father, mother, or friend) while making their decisions. In contrast, Asai's scale was created to specifically measure participants' Ibasho and the results were calculated from the sum of the four subscales. Since the reliability and factor validity of the scale had been examined in a previous study, we used the original scale and factors in our study. We measured participants' Ibasho using a 5-point scale ranging from 1 = disagree to 5 = agree. Our survey included 20 items, such as "I have a place where I can express myself as I am," "I am useful to someone," and "I have a person who accepts me unconditionally."

Results and Discussion

We compared the participants' scale scores before and after the collaborative construction task using a paired t-test. The t-test revealed that the scores for Ibasho (the sum of the four subscales) after the task were higher compared to the scores before the exercise ($t(19) = -1.81$, $p < .10$). In order to determine how the Ibasho was influenced by the collaborative construction exercise, we also compared the scores for each of the subscales to each other. These analyses revealed that the scores for the sense of roles significantly increased after the construction task ($t(19) = -3.18$, $p < .01$), whereas there was no significant difference between the sense of authenticity ($t(19) = 0.71$, *n.s.*), sense of perceived acceptance ($t(19) = -1.14$, *n.s.*), or the sense of relief ($t(19) = 0.66$, *n.s.*).

The results in this experiment indicated that collaborative self-expression through the use of LEGO® blocks increased the participants' general Ibasho. The participants communicated using both verbal and nonverbal means. Although the general Ibasho and the sense of role scores significantly increased after the task, there was no significant change in the other aspects of Ibasho (the sense of authenticity, the sense of perceived acceptance, and the sense of relief).

When the participants expressed themselves while working with others (such as in the block construction task), they all naturally assumed different roles and they were usually able to sense their particular responsibilities in each role. For example, in our study, when the individual participant's ideas for how to use the LEGO® blocks was accepted by the others in their group, it enhanced the participant's self-confidence and had a positive influence on how much they valued their roles. Ochiai and Sato (1996) examined whether there were gender differences for friendship styles in Japanese adolescents. They found that the level of both self-disclosure and the ability to understand one another were significantly higher in female adolescents than in male adolescents. Such aspects are important for maintaining healthy relationships and they serve as the basis for establishing roles in peer groups. We also found that these two features (self-disclosure and the ability to understand one another) were crucial for communication among the participants in this study.

Finally, the sense of role-playing also involved social skills. As described in previous sections, constructing a collaborative block creation increases social skills and allows for the establishment of roles among the participants. In our study, the sense of authenticity, perceived acceptance, and sense of relief did not increase as the sense of role-playing increased. Even though individual traits or personalities could be influenced by such factors, they did not change in the short term. Therefore, we believe that it is important for future researchers to examine the collaborative framework over a longer period of time in order to clarify the effects of these other factors on Ibasho.

In this study, we examined how a collaborative task could increase Ibasho. The findings indicated that the participants' sense of roles within groups was developed throughout the task, and this indicated that block creation collaborative tasks could be both effective mediums of communication in group settings and an effective tool in group therapy. Although the findings in this study can provide guidance for future applications of the approach in the suggested settings, it is necessary to interpret our findings with caution because the sample size was small and the setting was predetermined. More specifically, since there were only female participants in this study, future researchers should focus on including both genders in their clinical groups. They should also try to include participants of various ages, different cultural backgrounds, and people who have been diagnosed with developmental disorders.

EXAMPLES OF PRACTICES FOR FURTHER APPLICATION

In this section, I will describe some examples of the clinical applications of collaborative block creation based on evidence mentioned in previous sections of this chapter. While this method is useful with several clinical subpopulations and ages, we focused specifically on the application of this approach for groups of children having developmental disorders and student counseling for international students.

As Legoff (2004) demonstrated, toy blocks are very attractive to children and act as useful materials in the evaluation of children with developmental disorders. His "LEGO® Therapy" method is well structured and is effective as a social skill training program for them. However, our "Block Technique" approach allows for more freedom in expression than other approaches, and it can also be applied in a group therapy setting for children with developmental disorders. We tested the collaborative creation approach with a group of ASD children. In this study, we created small groups of three to five children that met with one of the facilitators. The facilitators were teachers or clinical psychologists and they were responsible for implementing the collaborative creation approach. Although the participants tended to convey a very narrow range of expressions at the beginning, they gradually started to communicate and collaborate more with each other. This process proved effective for helping the participants increase their social skills, self-efficacy, and satisfaction. Kato et al. (2013b) showed that this activity also had positive effects on trust for ASD children. Currently, we are preparing to test this approach with a group that includes children with several developmental disorders such as ASD and ADHD. Although ASD children prefer to be alone and stay in their inner world, ADHD children are often interested in many different things and actively communicate with other members. The social differences between these two groups of children may be a good opportunity for the participants to communicate with each other. Of course, the facilitators will have to closely monitor the group dynamics, maintain a good atmosphere, and secure the framework of the approach in order to facilitate the communication effectively.

Another setting where this approach could be applied is in student counseling. No matter how common individual counseling is in this area, the group approach is also effective. We used the collaborative block creation approach with groups of international students. For these students, they had to both study their professions in a non-native tongue and live in unfamiliar environments. Therefore, they were more likely to have language difficulties and feel isolated during the study of their majors. The group approach is effective in preventing these problems and can provide them a place where they can communicate with other students. These findings led us to form a group called the "cross-cultural communication group," an encounter group where the members performed group activities together. The collaborative block creation was included as one of the group activities. The small group included three to five Japanese students along with the facilitator. The process of creation was the same as what was used in previous studies, where students expressed themselves using only blocks and figures. In Kato et al. (2010), the group included both Japanese and Indonesian students. However, the members created houses and vehicles alone and there was very little collaboration between each member. One of them created a river on the center of the plate and this became a turning point for the entire group. After that, another member proposed to build a bridge across the river and the others built upon that idea. As they continued interaction with each other, they decided to create a town around the river. They shared their own images through these processes and their communications were facilitated. We also found that members gradually became more talkative through the course of the process. Since many of the members could not speak either perfect English or Japanese, it would not be unusual if they were hesitant to talk with other group members. We found that the group members found it easier to talk to each other through collaborative creation. We considered this communication important because their roles were divided naturally and they were satisfied with their own roles throughout the process. In addition, the participants experienced moments of proposal and acceptance during their collaborations. For instance, one proposed to create a bridge and the others accepted his opinion. This approach to communication is important in order to maintain social skills and increase the sense of being accepted by others.

In this chapter, I described how some groups used the collaborative block creation approach and how they may have had positive psychological effects on the participants. Therefore, based on our findings with groups of children with developmental disorders and international student counseling sessions, we expect more researchers to test the collaborative approach with other types of groups. In conclusion, the collaborative block creation proved to be a very useful type of group therapy with several different clinical subpopulations.

REFERENCES

Amagai,Y. (1995). The effect of trust on ego-identity of high school students. *Japanese Journal of Educational Psychology*, 43, 364–371.

Asai, M. (2013). Sense of Ibasho in Japanese female university students, Annual Report of Graduate School of Human Ecology, *Kinjo Gakuin University*, 13, 29–32.

Imagawa, M., Ohnishi, M., Yamaguchi, N., and Nakai, H. (1985). Block composition by schizophrenic patients after conventional psychotherapy sessions and its significance. *Japanese Bulletin of Arts Therapy*, 16, 41–46.

Irie, S. and Ohmori, K. (1991). A case of selective mutism: Using the LEGO blocks and sandplay techniques. *Japanese Bulletin of Arts Therapy*, 22(1), 50–60.

Ishimoto, Y. (2010). The influence of a sense of Ibasho on psychological and school adjustment in adolescence and emerging adulthood. *The Japanese Journal of Developmental Psychology*, 21(3), 278–286.

Ishimoto, Y., Kukawa, M., Saito, S., Kaminaga, M., Norisada, Y., Higata, A., and Moriguchi, R. (2009). Relations between friendship styles, psychological adjustment, and school adjustment among adolescent females. *The Japanese Journal of Developmental Psychology*, 20(2), 125–133.

Kalff, D. M. (1966). Sandspiel, seine therapeutische Wirkung auf die Psyche. Zürich: Rascher.

Kato, D., Asai, M., and Yoshie, M. (2013a). Effect of collaborative Lego® block construction on Japanese young women's sense of acceptance. *Social Behavior And Personality*, 41(8), 1333–1338.

Kato, D., Ogura, S., Nakazawa, S., Sasakawa, Y., and Morita, M. (2013b). A collaborative expression using blocks for students with high-Functioning pervasive developmental disorder. Treatises and Studies by the Faculty of Kinjo Gakuin University, *Studies in Humanities*, 10(1), 19–24.

Kato, D., Hattori, K., Iwai, S., and Morita, M. (2012). Effects of collaborative expression using LEGO® blocks, on social skills and trust. *Social Behavior And Personality,* 40(7), 1195–1200.

Kato, D., Takaki, H., Katsurada, Y., Hamada, S., and Wu, W. (2010). Collaborative expression using LEGO® blocks in cross cultural communication group. *Journal of International Student Advisors and Educators,* 12, 157–164.

Kato, D. (2006). A study of psychotherapy using blocks: Analysis of effects of the therapy by using POMS (Profile Of Mood States) and the relationship between the features of block works and mood states. *Japanese Bulletin of Arts Therapy,* 35(1,2), 52–62.

Kikuchi, A. (1988). Omoiyari wo kagaku suru [Science of sympathy]. Tokyo: Kawashima Shoten, Inc.

LeGoff, D. B. (2004). Use of Legos™ as a therapeutic medium for improving social competence. *Journal of Autism and Developmental Disorders,* 34(5), 557–571.

Norisada, Y. (2008). Developmental changes of "Ibasho" (one's psychological place) to significant others during adolescence. *The Japanese Journal of Counseling Science,* 41(1), 64–72.

Ochiai, Y. and Sato, Y. (1996). The developmental change of friendship in adolescence. *Japanese Journal of Educational Psychology*, 44, 55–65.

Owens, G., Granader, Y., Humphrey, A., and Baron-Cohen, S. (2008). LEGO® Therapy and the Social Use of Language Programme: An evaluation of two social skills interventions for children with high functioning autism and Asperger syndrome, *Journal of Autism and Developmental Disorders,* 38, 1944–1957.

Resnick, R. J. (1976). Block playing as a therapeutic technique. *Psychotherapy: Theory, Research and Practice*, 13(2), 170–172.

Roos, J., and Victor, B. (1999). Towards a model of strategy making as Serious Play, *European Management Journal*, 17(4), 348–355.

Roos, J., and Victor, B. (1998) In search of original strategies: how about some Serious Play? *IMD Perspectives for Managers*, 26, 15.

Turner, J. C., Hogg, M. A., Oakes, P. J., Reicher, S. D. and Wetherell, M. S. (1987). Rediscovering the social group: A self-categorization theory. Oxford: Blackwell.

Yli-Piipari, S., Kiuru, N., Jaakkola, T., Liukkonen, J., and Watt, A. (2011). The role of peer groups in male and female adolescents' task values and physical activity. *Psychological Reports*, 108(1), 75–93.

In: Group Therapy
Editor: Hellen Derrickson

ISBN: 978-1-63463-173-0

Chapter 6

THE EFFECT OF EFT (EMOTIONAL FREEDOM TECHNIQUES) ON SOCCER PERFORMANCE

Tam Llewellyn-Edwards PhD *

and B. A. Mary Llewellyn-Edwards

ABSTRACT

This study involved the use of a short session of Emotional Freedom Techniques (EFT) with two English ladies soccer teams.

It is a randomised controlled trial with a supporting uncontrolled trial.

It was designed to verify the results of an earlier similar American trial involving basketball players.

The results show a significant improvement in goal scoring ability from a dead ball situation following a short EFT session. These results support those of the earlier trial.

Keywords: Soccer, Performance, Emotional Freedom Techniques (EFT), anxiety, Stress

* Contact via TLlewellyn@AoL.com.

INTRODUCTION

There have been many studies on the effect of Emotional Freedom Techniques (EFT) and other Energy Psychology (EP) therapies on psychological conditions, including depression, anxiety, phobias and post-traumatic stress disorder. [1] However, even though significant success in the use of this therapy with individual elite athletes have been reported in individual cases [2-4] there have been few statistically valid studies.

A number of athletes in a variety of sports have reported large gains in performance after using EFT [10, 11]

One statistically valid study which did investigate the effect of EFT on a group of athletes (Basketball players) was that by Church. [5] This current study is an attempt to confirm the results of that study independently and using athletes from a different sport (Ladies' Soccer).

EFT was developed by Gary Craig as an abbreviation of the methods used in Thought Field Therapy (TFT), an earlier Energy Psychology Therapy developed by Callahan. [6] EFT's standardised procedure entails tapping on the end points of the acupuncture meridians while concentrating on the problem. [7] A full explanation of the procedure can be found in the *EFT Manual* [8] A free shortened version of this manual is available on the Net [9]

In the present study a group of female soccer players were tested for their ability to score a goal from a dead ball situation before and after they had received a ten minute group session of EFT which was aimed at stress reduction and the removal of emotional blocks against doing well at this task. A control group was also tested and they received conventional coaching while the active group received EFT help. No attempt was made to make the experiment blind

METHOD

Participants

Participants in this study were players of "Keepmoat Stadium Ladies", a group of female soccer teams for which the authors provide psychological coaching. This being the case the participants were familiar with EFT and had had some experience in its use and advantages and this made a blind test impossible.

Procedure

The study was carried out during normal practice sessions at The Keepmoat Stadium, Doncaster, United Kingdom using a small five-aside outdoor pitch where the teams usually trained. Informed consent had been obtained prior to the trails and they were undertaken with the support of the team management who provided two trainers to work with the control group.

A total of twenty-six players took part from the open and under 16 teams. Fifteen players from the senior team took part (Eight of these made up the control group). The age range of this group was 15 to 30. Eleven under 16 players made up a separate active group, all aged 14 to 15. The two age groups were studied separately, but the results are shown both individually and pooled. The control group was draw only from the senior team being judged to be those who would best benefit from the standard coaching procedures, whereas the under 16 girls were considered less likely to benefit from such a short standard coaching session. Thus the investigation could be described as being in two parts – a randomised controlled trial with the Open ladies and a supporting uncontrolled train with the under 16 girls.

All participants performed their usual warming-up period and then had the process of the trial explained to them.

The test involved taking two sets of five dead-ball kicks at goal from a distance of 13.5 metres. The goal was the standard 5-aside goal (5.0 meters wide by 1.2 metres high). There was no goalkeeper employed (to reduce the uncontrolled variables), but only kicks which entered in the two outer thirds of the available goal area were counted as scoring. Those which entered the centre third of the goal were considered as would have been saved by the 'goal keeper" After the first ten kicks the players were given a short coaching session and then 10 more kicks were to be taken. The trial was to assess if the coaching sessions served to make a significant improvement in performance, not to assess the performance of the individual players.

The fifteen senior payers were randomly divided into two groups – active and control. The control and active groups were sent to opposite ends of the pitch, but were intentionally allowed to watch the attempts of others to score. The under-16 group undertook the trail at a different time, but under identical conditions except that there was no under-16 control group.

Each player was allowed five kicks at goal, a short rest and five further kicks. The total of two attempts of ten kicks was selected after the participants trainers had judged that 20 kicks would not tire the players unduly. This trainers' estimate was halved to remove possible fatigue as an uncontrolled variable. The scores of the active teams were recorded by the authors and those of the control groups by two of the trainers.

Treatment Intervention

Once the ten initial goal shots had been taken the groups were given coaching in an attempt to increase their score rates. The active groups were give a coaching session by the authors which consisted of a group 'Borrowing Benefits' EFT session. This involved a group tapping session while they each considered what may have hindered their scoring in the earlier session as well as hearing the reasons expressed by others in their group. The control group had a group session with their normal trainers which were aimed at increasing their score rate. This involved the trainers commenting on the players earlier efforts at scoring and advising on actions to improve the ladies; technique in shooting. No actual shooting practice was allowed during this intervention.

Post-treatment Testing

After the coaching sessions the groups were again given two sets of five kicks at goal under identical condition to those used pre-treatment. Again the scoring level was recorded. The score rates before and after treatment for each group were compared and statistically assessed to judge if any improvement following treatment was significant and to compare the significance of any difference between the active groups and the control group.

RESULTS

The scoring rates in the first and second series of penalty kicks were calculated to determine the amount of improvement before and after coaching with EFT (Active groups) and normal coaching (Control Group). With this small sample it was not possible to test the results to see if they were normally distributed. Consequently the significance of the results was first assessed using a simple 'Sign Test' using the Null Hypothesis that the EFT Process did not significantly improve the players' performance when compared to the improvement from standard coaching. As the experiment produced numerical values for the performance change The 'Wilcoxon Signed Rank Sum Test' was used to increase the power of the testing. To facilitate comparison of the results with the earlier Church Study two-tailed t-tests were also undertaken The full test results are given in the attached Appendix. The results of the 'Sign Test' showed that the difference between their performance before and after coaching/EFT was significant in the "Open Ladies" active group, but not significant in the control group. As the under 16 sample size was larger this was not assessed using the 'Sign Test", but only using a t-test. All three groups, Control, Ladies Open and under 16 were assessed using a 't-test to judge if there was a significant difference before and after coaching against the Null Hypothesis that there would be no significant difference in performance.

This assessment showed:

- Control Group: T-value = 2.10, Calculated T-value = 0.31 Null hypothesis not rejected
- Ladies Open: T-value = 2.10, Calculated T-value = 2.20 Null hypothesis rejected
- Under 16: T-value = 2.10, Calculated T-value = 2.68 Null hypothesis rejected
- Pooled: T-value = 2.10, Calculated T-value = 2.95 Null hypothesis rejected

DISCUSSION

It was not expected or intended that the EFT coaching would improve the technical ability of the subjects to score, but rather that it would reduce the anxiety of the subjects about their ability to score in front of those who were observing their efforts. The influence of anxiety may account for the unexpected poorer result with the control group after standard coaching. The coaching session with their trainers may have increase the anxiety over their performance leading the poorer results. This fall off in performance was also observered in [5]. Most earlier investigations into the effectiveness of EFT have involved its use in conjunction with psychological distress although a few have evaluated its use to improve sports performance and there are a number of reported cases involving the performance of single athletes [12]

With regard to this investigation he most important earlier investigation is that by Church mentioned earlier [5]. That investigation involved the assessment of the improvement in performance by a group of basketball players following EFT coaching. This earlier investigation showed a statistically significant improvement following EFT and the performance increased by 20.8% for the active group, while decreasing by 16.6% for the control group. This current investigation supports these results completely. The active groups showed an increase in scoring rate of 40% and 45%, whereas the control group suffered an decrease of 4%.

A limitation of this study is its small sample size (pooled n = 18). The statistical measures used here are intended to compensate for the individual variances. When analysing these small samples, t-tests and "Sign Tests" were used and the tests chosen for the analysis fall within the parameters of the statistical tests used. However, replication of the investigation using a larger sample size is required to show if the results are typical.

Studies of non-athlete populations note a decrease in stress after EFT, with the gains being maintained on follow up investigation [13]. Outcome studies of EFT in clinical settings have shown a large effect size and efficacy in a wide variety of Psychological conditions [1]. Studies of physiological markers of stress, such as levels of the stress hormone cortisol, have demonstrated improvement after EFT treatment.

The results of this present study are consistent with the research showing that treatment of emotional memories with EFT produces physiological improvements

CONCLUSION

Clinical reports and accounts from coaches and athletes note that EFT is practiced in professional and amateur level golf, baseball, American football and soccer. This study, in conjunction with that of Church[(5)], indicates that a very brief application of EFT, administered in a very short time-scale can increase the performance of high-performing athletes. The use of EFT for stress reduction in sports warrants further empirical evaluation. Further study is required to determine if longer courses of EFT can produce still greater improvements. This study confirms the results previously found by Church[(5)] and opens up new potential applications for Energy Psychology. In that season, the under 16 Team were never beaten so just after the halfway point in the matches to be played they were champions in their league. The Under 16 striker scored more goals than had ever been scored in a season before and was given a special prize. The Open team came second in their league – higher than they had ever been placed.

ACKNOWLEDGMENTS

Thanks must go to the players of Keepmoat Stadium Ladies soccer teams, who took part in this study and gave up part of their valuable training time to undertake the trials. Special thanks must be given to Eric Randerson, Community Chief Executive of Doncaster Rovers Football Club (who is also head coach of Keepmote Stadium Ladies Open Team) who gave permission for this trial to go ahead and provided facilities, and to Julie Jay, Head Coach of Keepmote Stadium Ladies under 16 team for their help and encouragement.

Thanks must also go to Gary Craig who developed EFT and who trained the authors in its techniques. Thanks also to all those colleagues who helped the authors develop their skills in this area, and especial thanks to Dawson Church of EFT-Universe who encouraged the authors to undertake the study and helped in the design of the trial

RESULTS APPENDIX

Control Group

TEST	BEFORE	AFTER
Subject 1	4.00	7.00
Subject 2	6.00	6.00
Subject 3	8.00	3.00
Subject 4	7.00	6.00
Subject 5	8.00	9.00
Subject 6	5.00	5.00
Subject 7	7.00	7.00
Subject 8	7.00	7.00
Average	**6.50**	**6.25**

Calculated T-value = 0.31 (Not Significant)

Ladies Open Group

TEST	BEFORE	AFTER
Subject 1	7.00	9.00
Subject 2	7.00	6.00
Subject 3	3.00	6.00
Subject 4	2.00	7.00
Subject 5	6.00	6.00
Subject 6	6.00	8.00
Subject 7	6.00	9.00
Average	**5.29**	**7.29**

Calculated T-Value = 2.20 (Significant)

Under 16 Group

TEST	BEFORE	AFTER
Subject 1	5.00	7.00
Subject 2	6.00	7.00
Subject 3	3.00	6.00
Subject 4	4.00	8.00
Subject 5	2.00	3.00
Subject 6	8.00	7.00
Subject 7	4.00	6.00
Subject 8	2.00	9.00
Subject 9	4.00	5.00
Subject 10	5.00	5.00
Subject 11	6.00	8.00
Average	**4.45**	**6.45**

Calculated T-value = 2.68 (Significant)

Pooled Results

TEST	BEFORE	AFTER
Subject 1	5.00	7.00
Subject 2	6.00	7.00
Subject 3	3.00	6.00
Subject 4	4.00	8.00
Subject 5	2.00	3.00
Subject 6	8.00	7.00
Subject 7	4.00	6.00
Subject 8	2.00	9.00
Subject 9	4.00	5.00
Subject 10	5.00	5.00
Subject 11	6.00	8.00
Subject 12	7.00	9.00
Subject 13	7.00	6.00
Subject 14	3.00	6.00
Subject 15	2.00	7.00
Subject 16	6.00	6.00
Subject 17	6.00	8.00
Subject 18	9.00	9.00
Average	**4.94**	**6.78**

Calculated t-value = 2.95 (Significant)

Before /After Comparison

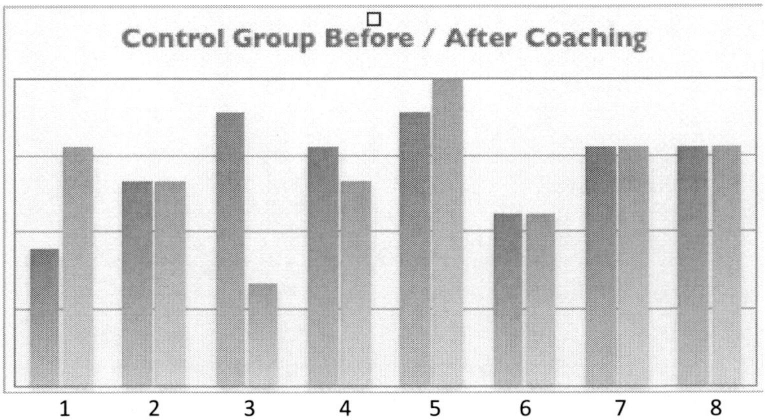

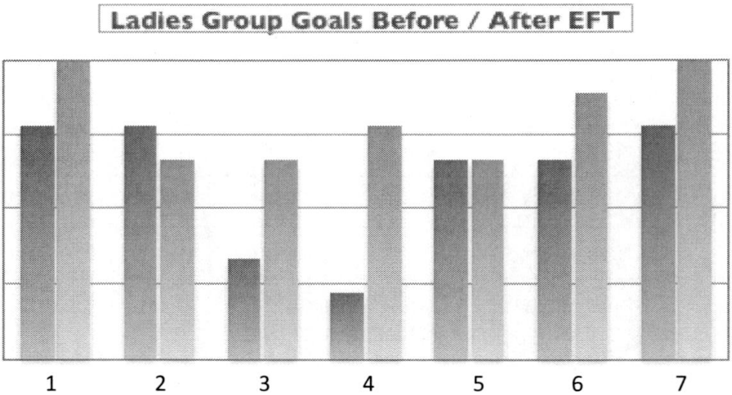

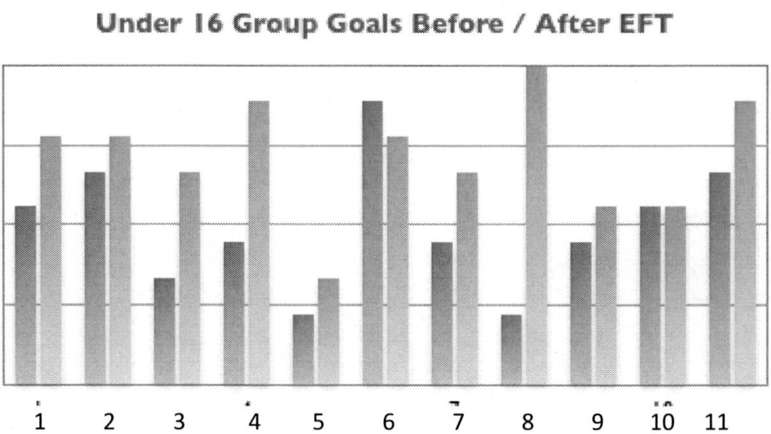

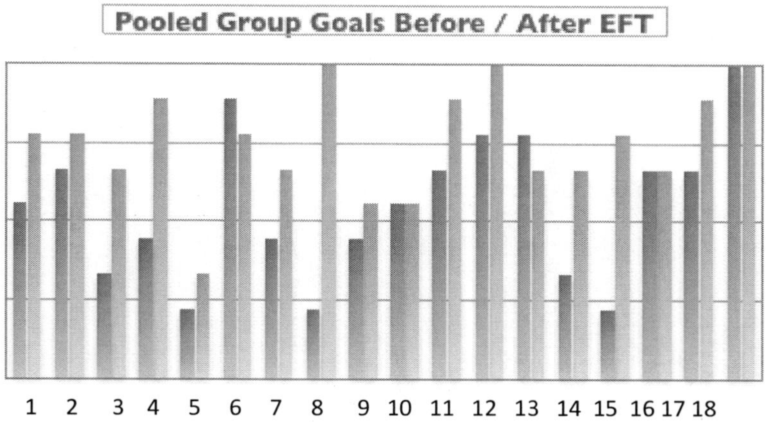

REFERENCES

[1] Feinstein, D: "Energy Psychology-A Review of the Preliminary Evidence": *Psychother Theory Res Prac Train* 2008; 45(2): 199-213.

[2] Achenbach, J: "Golfers 'Tap" into Psychology": Golfweek 2007; 25:60.

[3] Borzi, P: "Beavers 11, Tar Heels 4- Oregon State one win from a second title": New York Times 2007, June 24 (Available from http://query.nytimes.com).

[4] Crist, R: "Elite Athletes & Amateurs alike are continually searching for Things that can help the attain Peal Performance": Scottdale Republic 2005.

[5] Church, D: "The Effect of EFT(REmotional Freedom Techniques) on Athletic performance – A Randomised Controlled Blind Trial." *Open Sports Science Journal* 2009; 2: 94-99.

[6] Calahan, R: *"Tapping the Healer Within: Using Thought Field Therapy....."* New York: McGraw-Hill 2000.

[7] Feinstein, D et al.: *"The Promise of Energy Psychology"* New York: Thatcher 2005: p 108.

[8] Craig, G: *"The EFT Manual (2nd Ed)"* Energy Psychology Press 2011

[9] Craig, G: "The EFT Mini Manual" (Available from http://www.eftuniverse.com).

[10] Rowe, J: *"EFT and Golf"* Bangor, ME: Booklocker 2009.

[11] EFT Power Training. (Available from http://www.eftpowertraining.com)

[12] Craig, G: "EFT for Sports Performance" Energy Psychology Press 2101.
[13] Rowe, J:"The Effects of EFT on long-term Psychological Symptoms. *Counsel Clinical Psychology Journal* 2005: 2(3): 104-111.

INDEX

C

D

E

F

G

H

M

N

O

P

Q

R

S

T